A LIFE THAT MATTERS

A LIFE THAT MATTERS

Autobiographical Essays of a Filipino Activist

Rey Abaya

authorHOUSE®

AuthorHouse™
1663 Liberty Drive
Bloomington, IN 47403
www.authorhouse.com
Phone: 1-800-839-8640

First published by AuthorHouse   10/27/2009

ISBN: 978-1-4490-4033-8 (e)
ISBN: 978-1-4490-4031-4 (sc)
ISBN: 978-1-4490-4032-1 (hc)

Library of Congress Control Number: 2009911044

Printed in the United States of America
Bloomington, Indiana

This book is printed on acid-free paper.

To
Mario my soulmate
and
Del my lifemate

TABLE OF CONTENTS

PART 1:
INTRODUCTORY ESSAY

CHAPTER I

THE ACTIVIST PERSPECTIVE

Last night I spent three hours phone banking for the gubernatorial candidacy of Phil Angelides. At the time I am writing this, Phil is running against the sitting governor of California, Arnold Schwarzenegger, a celebrity cinema action star . As I write this, it is now less than thirty days before the November 7, 2006 election, but Phil is still trailing badly in the polls. I think he is the much better candidate of the two, but many of his supporters have already given up on him. Last night, there were only two of us phone banking at the union office. The other phone banker was Gabe, a temporary political representative hired by our union. Even with the discouraging polls, I have not given up on Phil's candidacy so I volunteer to phone bank on Tuesdays and Wednesdays when I am not feeling too tired from my regular work.

It is during times like last night that I truly feel spiritually replenished because that kind of work really tests my resolve to keep on fighting despite overwhelming odds. The temptation to just give up and go home like the rest of humanity can become so overwhelming and emotionally debilitating that staying on despite what I feel can only make me feel stronger spiritually. I keep reminding myself that the world needs people like me to persevere in this difficult and thankless work because I really make a difference. *Perseverance moves mountains.* I keep reminding myself that in 2000, President Bush squeaked by Al Gore by a mere 500 or so votes, and what a difference it had made on the lives of many Americans. The difference in this contest might be 50 people like me who have not yet thrown in the towel.

It is not easy to call other people's phones and intrude on them during their leisure time to talk about the election and about how important it is for them. Less than twelve percent actually pick up to answer their phones. Among the live ones whom I might catch actually picking up their phone, about a fourth will give me a nasty piece of their mind. I often feel like an unwelcome intruder stealing a few minutes of their rest period. I understand that people are protective of their private lives. They are usually outraged that I dare to bother them after their hard day's work. Thus rebuked, I just swallow my pride and try to be pleasant and understanding. Once in a while, I get a welcome bonus in the form of an admiring compliment or a grateful acknowledgment of my volunteer effort. Even in the midst of their self-absorption, one or two people understand what I am doing. That makes my day.

I ride an emotional roller coaster during the three hours of phone banking, going through a range of emotions, from discouragement and despair to satisfaction and exhilaration. There is no financial compensation, and I expect none, but there is definitely a reward: my spiritual growth. I feel a certain maturing after every phone banking session. The heartaches and the letdowns serve as spiritual supplements for the true believer in activism. They strengthen the soul of the activist in a more significant way than if he had gone to church and attended services there. The phone banking halls and the precinct-walking streets are the arenas where the activist's character is forged. One learns self-discipline with every insult he takes without rancor, sporting an almost Spartan disregard for his own ego.

The activist is a very spiritual man but in a much different way than the usual religious person. He believes that the spiritual nature of man is shaped not through constant prayer but through constant action. Actions speak louder than words or prayers because in the realm of reality, words are cheap, and actions are much more difficult to do. Actions prove to the people around us the values that we profess to believe in. Most of us do not really confront the veracity of what we publicly say we believe in until we have to do something in line with those beliefs at some personal cost to us.

What we do from Monday to Saturday is the essence of our spirituality, not what we profess on Sunday in community. Sunday is the culmination of our "holy" week when we bring to our community the vessels that we are---empty, half-full, or full---to offer to the deity we profess to believe in. If we do not do anything good from Monday to Saturday, there seems to be no point for us to attend the celebration on Sunday because we come as empty vessels without anything to bring as sacrifice. There is no faith to celebrate because our faith is hollow; the values we profess to believe in have not been validated by actions in the real world.

This is not to say that phone banking and precinct walking are necessary for salvation. These are just some activities that activists can do. What I want to say is that activism is necessary for salvation. We cannot go through life without actively practicing the values we say we believe in and expect to be saved. There are a myriad of things that we can do to make the world a better place, *to help build a heaven on this earth.* Everyone must help if everyone expects to be saved.

The opportunity for us to help solve some problem in the real world will always present itself. I call this God's gift. It manifests itself constantly. We only have to be open to its revelation. These opportunities are all around us, waiting to be exploited by us. That is why I call them gifts. We are doubly blessed when we use them. We feel the exhilaration of participating in God's creative energy in transforming this world into a better one; *the energy of the immanent God flows through us.* It also brings us nearer to our self-understanding of what we are destined to be, what the Buddhists call " an enlightened one". If one is a Christian, Jesus had already shown him the way through the values he taught him through the New Testament. These values are simple and unmistakably clear. The rituals must not be mistaken for the values, such that we love the rituals and throw out the values, missing the essential because of attention to form.

Although I have had experience of the contemplative life when I entered the novitiate in my teenage years to spend a year mostly in silence doing work and silent meditation, I feel I am not really cut out for the contemplative life. I see myself as a man of action, constantly experimenting with real things to effect real results. My activist life in a way is a prayer in itself, a constant reaffirmation of the things I believe in.

For me, combing my hair is the key moment of every day because it is judgment time; I face myself without shame and regret, assuring myself that I have kept my integrity intact, despite what other people may think of me. That, for me, is the only real value. Everything else is chaff.

PART 2: ROOTS

CHAPTER 2

SOULMATE

I knew Mario from our kindergarten days. He was this buck-teethed, nerdy-looking, slightly built boy who was the perfect fit for the role of Ichabod Crane in The Legend of Sleepy Hollow. At our young age when small boys regard physical achievements very highly, he definitely looked unimpressive to me. Although we were classmates, we were not close friends then.

Despite his physical limitations, young Mario liked to join the usual rough games of active small boys, like fencing with bamboo swords and engaging in mock land battles using rubber slingshots as firearms and folded paper as bullets. What he lacked in physical prowess he made up for in smartness. He would, with the slyness of Loki, make sure that some older, and therefore bigger, ally always protected him, acting as his personal bodyguard. His usual protector was Tito, a classmate who was a year older than both of us and bigger than everybody else in the class.

Wielding influence over a few of our peers was easy for Mario, as his parents were powerful people in our small town. His mother, a judge in a neighboring town, was the eldest child of the wealthiest landowner in our town. His father was a foreman in the local public highways office, an influential man with legions of construction workers reporting to him, just a notch below the district engineer in rank.

Mario and I belonged to the two elite clans of our small town, the de Veyra and Villegas clans.

In my case, although my mother and her older sister were ordinary elementary school teachers, they were regarded highly by the town. Their older brother was the academic superintendent of the school district, managing all the public schools of some fifty towns in the area. Their father, my grandfather who died during the Second World War, was mayor of our town for two terms just before the Second World War; he was also the titular head of the second-largest clan in the town, the Villegas clan. My father was not from our town, originating from a distant area in the northern part of the Philippines known as the Ilocos region. He came to our town just before the Second World War as a young geodetic engineer employed by the Philippine government and assigned to conduct surveys in our town. As a non-native professional working for the government, he had some stature in the community, and several young men of the town were working for him. Mario's clan, the de Veyra clan, was the largest and most influential in our town.

Mario and I were born a few years after the Second World War, in a town that still showed the scars of General MacArthur's grand campaign to retake the Philippines from the Japanese. Relentless bombing runs were a prelude to his historic landing on the beaches of our province Leyte. Our town Tanauan took the brunt of the air and sea shelling. Empty torpedo shells as well as unexploded bombs lay everywhere in our vicinity. War stories told by our parents were fresh and vivid. Douglas MacArthur was everyone's bigger-than-life hero for the promise he kept to liberate the Philippines; the Japanese were the hated bogeymen, cruel masters of a recent dark age. In our childhood, the wounds of war had not yet fully healed.

Although as young kids we grew up in the same small town, our houses a stone's throw from each other, Mario and I were not particularly close. We were classmates in kindergarten, grade four, and again in grade five, but those were the only times we were in the same class before high school. After grade six, Mario went away to enter the Catholic seminary in a neighboring town while I enrolled at the local high school, a private Catholic school.

Our paths crossed again a year later, in our sophomore year, when we enrolled in the same seminary in the country's capital city Manila, along with my then closest friend Eugene. Apparently, the same recruiters that convinced Eugene and me to try seminary life had also persuaded Mario to transfer from his seminary to the same one Eugene and I had chosen. Mario came as a regular second year student while Eugene and I were accepted as special students who had to take two years of Latin in one year.

In the seminary, four of us who came from the same place were classmates in the same class; we became inseparable companions. Ninong, who came from a neighboring town, joined our group of Mario, Eugene, and myself. We spoke the same *Waray* dialect, and having similar common experiences, we created our own smaller subculture amidst the more dominant groups of Cebuanos, Tagalogs, and Ilokanos. As a minority group that the larger groups casually dismissed and marginalized, we felt we needed to band together to survive. In the few times when we were forced by circumstances to mix with a major group in the seminary, our small group chose to blend in with the Tagalogs as we felt more comfortable with them.

During summer vacations, seminarians like us tended to stick together all the time in our hometowns. Seminary authorities specifically instructed us before summer vacation not to mix with girls, even our sisters' friends, to avoid getting involved with the opposite sex. We had to avoid girls like the plague. *Celibacy was an issue that overshadowed everything in our life.* At the start of vacation, we had to present ourselves to the town's parish priest to be accounted for. At the end of vacation, the parish priest had to accomplish a checklist about our behavior during vacation that we had to turn in to the seminary authorities upon return. We usually ended up spending summer vacation totally in the company of other seminarians, isolated from the rest of the community. We felt like outcasts, unable to relate to anybody except people like ourselves, like members of a chosen but untouchable caste. By force of circumstances then, other seminarians from our hometown became our closest friends. We shared the same hopes, the same visions, the same stories, even the same anxieties.

Free-spirited Eugene was the first to leave the seminary, after third year high school, probably feeling stifled by the rigorous regimen of seminary life. Athletic-minded Ninong followed, leaving after fourth year high school, succumbing to the lure of the pretty girls in his neighborhood. Serious and determined but feeling more and more isolated, Mario and I stuck it out together. Although we had other friends in the seminary during the regular school year, it was pretty much just Mario and I during summer break after Eugene's and Ninong's departures. We came to dread summer because it meant being in a smaller, lonelier social world.

We tried to buoy up our spirits through endless dialogues of the mind. Our conversations were never stale nonetheless. We somehow managed to stay focused and excited. We discussed many interesting topics, never veering away into topics about the opposite sex, although it was always tantalizingly just beneath the surface. That subject was taboo, and we obediently adhered to that rule. We talked of other things, and that was how we managed to survive, by intellectualizing almost everything within our purview. For the greater part of our waking lives, we learned to live in our minds, through our minds. Notwithstanding our artificially sanitized world, we nevertheless lived vibrant and exciting lives in our active minds, in the unending discussions that we looked forward to, day in and day out. Discourse became our specialty. We became brothers in the mind, *soul mates*, where one could finish the other's sentence and be almost always correct. It was quite comforting to know that there was another mind in this world that could understand and explain one's deepest thoughts in much the same way he could.

As we waged what loomed as a long, fourteen-year struggle to survive and ultimately become a priest, we fought our fiercest battles together in the limited confines of the seminary. Life that could have been boring became actually exciting as we embarked on our own crusade.

The period was the later part of the 1960s, the years after Vatican Council II when so many things were exciting, and everything seemed to be in flux within the Catholic Church. We were part of a big class of forty-four seminarians in a seminary of some two hundred seminarians, and we regarded our class as a crusading army. Much like the warrior generals of the past that we had read about, we savored leading the attacks on the increasingly meaningless structures and strictures of the institution we were in. The battles, always exciting, were not always self-satisfying. There were many instances when close friends betrayed us. We did not always win.

It was during this period when Mario and I learned that we could trust each other unconditionally. We vindicated all the days we had spent together discussing, probing, and exploring. Many times, it was just the two of us left to wage battle for our ideas. We were Don Quixote and Sancho Pancha battling the windmills of our hopes and dreams. Not once did he abandon me, and I always returned the favor.

As personalities, Mario and I were worlds apart. I was brash, speaking my mind with little tact and reservation. He was more calculating. I was all heart. He was more mental. I was fiery. He was cool. I riled and antagonized adversaries, appearing to be extremely combative. He intimidated them with the power of his words. I took pains to simplify complex things. He spoke to confuse and rattle. I spoke directly, without mincing words. He spoke with a sophistication that was deliberately cultivated to generate deference.

I did not survive the long trek to the priesthood.

In my constant fight for meaning and relevance, I antagonized superiors and peers, making my presence in the community untenable. The authorities expelled me from the seminary after I had spent ten years of my life in its confines. In many of those years, I had constantly bucked the system, believing in the righteousness of my beliefs and in the ultimate fairness of the process. I pushed the system to its limits in my honest desire to change it from within, and I paid a stiff price. The expulsion was the culmination of my personal crusade to become an activist priest completely dedicated to the poor, a campaign that failed to achieve the target. I disappointed my mother who was my chief supporter and my father who was my chief critic.

I am proud of that failure. I have never seen it any other way, deeming it a medal of valor earned in the greatest of my battlefields, a mortal wound sustained for courage of conviction. The way I saw it, I did not succumb, as others did, to the temptation of compromising just to get meaningless crumbs. I went for the meaningful but failed.

As if on cue, Mario did not lag far behind. Two days after my departure, Mario was knocking at the door of my sister's apartment where I was temporarily residing, proudly announcing that he had finally mustered the courage to leave the seminary. They had not dismissed him; he had dismissed himself. He told me he had long been besieged by doubts about his vocation, and according to him, my dismissal was the last argument that convinced him *the priesthood was not the place for him*. I was sad that our journey had ended. But I was also glad that my soul mate had again chosen to stand by me. His opinion was all I needed and cared for. He understood, and I was appeased.

Each armed with a master's degree in Philosophy, both of us initially went into teaching. Mario taught Philosophy at Saint Paul College and St. Theresa's College, both exclusive girls' schools in Manila. I taught at the College of the Holy Spirit, also an exclusive girls' school in Manila.

Our teaching stints were short-lived, however, as he was dismissed from St. Theresa's College after a year, while I was dismissed from the College of the Holy Spirit, also after a year. It was not because we were incompetent. The ratings the students gave us for teaching were the highest in our respective schools. We were bright, articulate, sympathetic, and competent. *Our students loved us.* But our reputation for stirring controversy in the seminary followed us to the colleges through the network of priests and nuns. The school authorities, mostly nuns, decided they were safer without us. They gave us lame excuses about why our services were no longer needed, but the real message was clear: they did not want trouble. By a strange twist, I applied to St. Theresa's College as Mario's replacement and was accepted, but that also was short-lived as they eventually found the link, and I was dismissed after one semester.

While I was teaching Philosophy at St. Theresa's College, Mario left Manila for Cebu, a city in the middle of the Philippines. For a while I lost contact with him. I was pleasantly surprised when one day a visitor,

Cynthia Banzon, whom I had met a year earlier when she and Mario visited me at the College of the Holy Spirit, came to see me at the school. She came to ask for the latest news on Mario, about whom I had no update, as well as to introduce Ric Manapat, a student of the Ateneo de Manila University. From what I gathered, Ric admired Mario quite a lot even though the two had not yet met. From my short conversation with Ric, I learned that Philosophy was his major at his school, which explained why he showed such uncanny interest in Mario. Mario had built a reputation among his former students of being a provocative Philosophy teacher. Cynthia was a former student of Mario who became his close friend.

I did not know it then but at about the time Cynthia and Ric visited me, Mario was in the custody of the government military in Cebu.

He had been conducting clandestine teach-ins there when the military apprehended him while driving a Volkswagen Kombi. According to Mario, they subsequently framed him by photographing him with a cache of guns that they supplied for the photo session but claimed to have found inside the van he was driving.

They blindfolded Mario, took him to the bathroom of a house they were using as a safe house for newly apprehended activists, ordered him to lie with his face down, with his eyes blindfolded, and left him there to ponder his fate for the next two days. One of his captors came back after two days, put a handgun to the side of his head, and pulled the trigger. Nothing happened. It was all part of psychological warfare, as the gun was not loaded. He said they did this for two consecutive days, then changed tactics.

The new tactic was more painful, although less horrifying. They placed hooks on his shoulder blades, connected the hooks to ropes that went over the beams near the roof, made him stand up so that he was in a tiptoe position, pulled on the ropes until they were taut, then finally tied the ropes to nearby posts so that he would be in an awkward position of not being able to relax his feet without hurting his shoulder blades. His captors would regularly come into the room to make sure that he maintained his awkward tiptoe position. Several times a day, they told him that they would kill him, but they never really carried it out. After several days of subjecting him to such grueling experience, they brought him to the camp for detainees, where they indefinitely held him without formally filing charges.

I came to know about his detention in Cebu from his mother who came to Manila to contact a mutual uncle who was a colonel in the government military and head of the country's crime laboratory. She sought me out looking for a picture of Mario. I steered her to a mutual friend from the seminary, Luke, who still had pictures of Mario from the time Luke was editor in chief of our high school yearbook. The picture was the last item our uncle needed to file an application for Mario's release from the Cebu detention camp to his custody in Manila. A few months later, Mario was back in circulation in Manila.

When I finally met him again, I told Mario about Cynthia Banzon's visit and Ric Manapat's interest in him. He got in touch with Ric Manapat, and it was this connection that led him to Sister Mary Mananzan and the College of St. Scholastica. Apparently, Ric was a very close friend of Sister Mary Mananzan, who was the dean of the college. Sister Mary offered Mario a teaching job at the college where he was appointed the chairman of the Philosophy department. I occasionally visited Mario at the College of St. Scholastica to discuss old issues and recent developments.

Mario developed his own circle of friends at the college while I went into business management. I pursued a master's degree in business administration at the De La Salle University while working as product manager at the marketing department of the Philippine

Refining Company, a subsidiary of the British multinational company, Unilever.

I received my master's degree in business administration in June 1979, after which I went back to part-time teaching at the college level, this time teaching business subjects.

Still keeping my day job at the Philippine Refining Company, I joined an all-male faculty teaching marketing subjects at an all-female school, the Philippine Women's University, along Taft Avenue in Manila. It was a welcome respite from the graduate education I had just finished, and it served to fill the time vacuum that suddenly was mine to spend as I pleased. It was also some sort of a recreation for me, socializing with girls eight years younger. Most of the girls were working students, going to work during the day and going to school after work to finish college. Hardly anybody had time to open books so listening to the teacher in class was their only source of knowledge about the subject matter. They were generally more liberal in their behavior than the girls I had previously taught at the Catholic colleges, probably because they were used to dealing with working young professionals and had fewer inhibitions about socializing. I found them more open in their relationship with the teachers and more enjoyable to teach because of their down-to-earth outlook. Although there were fewer academic standouts among them, I enjoyed the year I spent there more than any I had spent teaching elsewhere.

The next school year, Mario called to offer me two subjects to teach at St. Scholastica after work. He explained that he was in short supply of teachers for his department, and since I had already finished my MBA course, there was no reason I would not accept the assignment. I was actually glad to accept the teaching assignment because it meant I had more time to hook up with him again and continue the discussions that we both enjoyed. Besides, he gave me some leeway on how I would manage the syllabus of the course, which suited me quite well.

Mario introduced me to his circle of friends at the college. They were mostly his male faculty colleagues who were also his basketball buddies. In the seminary, Mario was not really into basketball as much as I was, but he was re-introduced to basketball during his stint as a faculty member at St. Scholastica. One of his basketball buddies was Jojo Binay who later became mayor of Makati during the Cory Aquino years. I was a part-time faculty member so occasionally I would join a basketball game or a friendly political discussion with his friends. Most of his friends were die-hard Marcos oppositionists, and a good number of them were members of MABINI, an association of opposition lawyers whose most notable leader was the venerable former senator Lorenzo Tanada.

I spent only one academic year with Mario at St. Scholastica. A multinational company recruited me to work for them in Jakarta, Indonesia, in the meantime, and in September 1981, I left for Indonesia.

During my working stint in Jakarta, I occasionally visited Manila a few weeks at a time. I did this in December 1983, December 1985, September 1987, August 1988, and July 1991. During those visits, I always spent a day or two with Mario, in their house or at St. Scholastica, resuming the conversations that were interrupted by my work in exile in Jakarta. It was not difficult restarting where we left off the last time. We were so familiar with each other's way of thinking that every conversation flowed so naturally. For me personally, continuing my interrupted conversation with Mario was the real reason for coming home. I did not have to be in Tanauan, the town of our birth and childhood, to be home. He was the one person that made me feel I was home because he evoked in me all the memories of what to me was a unique life that only he and I understood and savored.

I had an unexpected heart attack in March 1992, at the age of 43, while playing basketball with friends in Jakarta. When it happened, I was at the peak of my health and feeling indestructible, or so I thought. After that fateful heart attack, I was never the same again physically. Unknown to me, Mario had his own physical disaster that same year. In December 1992, he suffered an aneurysm of the brain to which he succumbed. He was pronounced DOA at the hospital.

I did not learn about Mario's demise at the time of his death. I came to know about it in June 1993 while I was visiting my mother and my siblings who had migrated to the United States.

At the time of Mario's death, my younger sister Cora learned about it from Angie, Mario's younger sister and Cora's close friend. The family had decided to keep the news from me because of my own health problems. They feared devastating news like that would aggravate whatever health problem I still had. During that visit, I started talking about my plans of going back to Tanauan and partnering with Mario in business. It was then that they decided they could not keep the news from me anymore. They tried to deliver it as gently as possible so that it would not shock me.

The full brunt of the news did not hit me until I was back in Jakarta sometime in July 1993, about the time of Mario's birthday. I wrote a letter to his wife Karina to explain that I could not send words of grief earlier as I had not known. Karina knows that among Mario's friends from his earlier life in the seminary, I was the closest. In fact, Mario had signified that by making me the godfather of one of his eldest twin daughters. I had never written a letter as poignant as the one I wrote to Mario's widow, and I kept a photocopy of that handwritten letter for my own file. I occasionally read it to remind myself about what he meant to me. I must have reopened wounds when Karina received it, but I felt I needed to tell her that I shared her loss of someone special.

I met Mario again a year afterwards, two days after my open-heart surgery, in a near-death experience. As I hovered between life and death in the intensive care unit, I saw him talking to me, but I could not hear his words. He seemed to be at the other side of what seemed to be a river, and I was craning my neck to understand what he was saying, but I still could not hear him. Then I woke up, covered with perspiration, but feeling certain that I was going to live.

I always thought of Mario and myself as twin books. I was the chronicle of his earlier life as much as he was the chronicle of my earlier life. Our wives were the chronicles of our later lives. As long as Mario was alive, somebody knew about me almost as comprehensively as I knew myself. With his passing, I became obsessed with my own mortality and the distinct possibility that everything about me would disappear when I die. I felt that I needed to explain a lot of things, at least to my children and grandchildren, to give them a sense of what I was to myself. Mario was no longer around to do it for me; I felt I had to do it myself.

It would take my vacation in 2008, after being away from Manila for some eleven years, to bring home to me the magnitude of my personal loss. I attended a class reunion of sort that eight other classmates also attended. We were discussing various topics, but I was feeling ill at ease, suddenly feeling the glaring absence of my sharp-tongued, usually next-chair buddy to whom, in such occasions, I would usually whisper some caustic remark at which we would roll our eyes together in understanding. I felt very lonely that night of our reunion, realizing that Mario was indeed gone forever.

This book is imbued with as much his spirit as with mine, a collaboration of sort dating back to our early years when we dared to battle the windmills of our youth.

CHAPTER 3

POSTER BOY

Iam my family's poster boy, the role model in the family that any family member could point to and feel proud of.

To my mother, I was the golden boy, education-wise, career-wise, and family-wise. Among her children, I was the most successful in school, always at the top of my class, and always making her and my father the envy of their peers because I constantly brought home academic medals and trophies. Career-wise, although I languished for a while in the slow lanes of the academe, I was finally able to get into the fast track when I was taken into the brand group of Unilever's detergents division where I learned on-the-job marketing. A stroke of good luck brought me to Jakarta, Indonesia, where my career as a business executive really took off and flourished. In the relative luxury of an expatriate manager's life, living in a big house with six big bedrooms, with three maids and two drivers at our disposal, my wife and I brought up our three children in an artificially sanitized world devoid of the anxieties of being poor. A subsequent prescient decision brought me to sunny California where my two older children distinguished themselves by doing well academically in high school and getting accepted to prestigious universities. As of this writing, my eldest is a senior at Stanford University while his younger brother is a junior at the University of Southern California. My youngest child is a 14-year old 8th grader, gymnast, swimmer, violinist, and academic achiever, all rolled into one, that exhibits the same intensity as her overachieving eldest brother in Stanford.

My mother was an elementary school teacher who, despite having to hold down a full time job, single-handedly brought up her seven children. That was quite a task. She had to earn money, do the disciplining, wash the clothes, and do all the other household chores that a housewife was expected to do. *She was the constant in our lives.* As far back as we could remember, she was always there in the vicinity looking over us, the strong-willed woman who could both inspire and terrify us. In fact, when she died at the ripe age of eighty-two, my three unmarried sisters and my divorced brother and his son were still living with her in her house. She was the one who instilled in us whatever values we managed to internalize in our growing years. *We are what our mothers formed us to be.*

My father was always in some other place doing surveying work. Being a field person, he was conspicuous for his constant absence from our house. When he was at home, he acted like a wealthy guest-relative, and we would have an abundance of nice things like exotic fruits, soft drinks, and even beer diluted in soda, all courtesy of his thick wallet. As his wallet thinned, his days at home would be numbered as he prepared for his work adventures elsewhere. My siblings and I knew very little about him as his presence was always fleeting, giving us little time to really know him as a person. He seemed to us more like Santa Claus whose presence we associated with nice things and enjoyable times.

My mother inspired me to think about doing great things in my lifetime. That was the reason I wanted to become a Catholic priest even as a small boy. She helped me nurture that desire, guiding me to concentrate on the things that really matter. We did not know it then, but when I needed to make the most difficult decisions later, the lessons I learned from her would continue to guide me. *One cannot fully fathom the wisdom of mothers.*

I was at the top of my class when I graduated from grade six, from high school, and from college. Nobody among my siblings matched that record. I was my mother's source of pride, and her peers envied her because of me. I thought that because I brought her the most in honor I deserved to be her favorite. But mothers are not like that. *Mothers don't give based on what they receive.* Only now that I am a parent myself can I understand it better.

I was one of two children in a brood of seven that did not bring my mother problems; both of us always tried to do the things she advised us to do and more. We never messed up, at home or in school. In my case, whenever relatives or acquaintances would ask my mother about me, she would refer to me as her good son, meaning, the son who did not go into tantrums, obliquely referring to my older brother in contrast.

When I left our family home at the age of twelve to enter the seminary in Manila, I felt ready to hold my own and mix it up with other families' children in an environment without families to console and support us. I continued to do well academically, much to my surprise, even in the midst of equally gifted children. Although I was the newly-arrived country bumpkin, I soon discovered I had more skills and was better prepared than most of my peers for life in the seminary. My competitive instincts served me well; before long, I was comfortably at the top of my class in academic achievement and never relinquished that place for the rest of my seminary term.

I became obsessed with academic achievement, and for a time, I lost my focus as to why I was in the seminary. (I was there to become a priest because I wanted to do great things in my lifetime.) As several years went by, the regularity of life in the seminary lulled us seminarians into a dreamlike stupor, caused by boredom, dulling our sense of purpose. I gradually woke up from that sleep, horrified that my life was destined to be one of daily rituals where as priest I would be *some rigid robot leading an equally uninspired community of people in orating senseless platitudes to an emotionless but demanding God.* I told myself that life had to be something more than that. I panicked. I had to find a more meaningful goal to tie my life to. Many of my peers just gave up, unable to rediscover their original sense of purpose. I however did not want to give up that easily.

As a church insider, the seminarian starts to notice a great disconnect between doing great things and being a Catholic priest. What the priest did on a daily basis did not seem much like doing great things. What becomes apparent is that a priest is a spinner of rituals and a great speaker of platitudes. The rituals and platitudes may calm the anxiety of churchgoing devotees, but just as equally they trouble the earnest priest-to-be. The more earnest one is, the more troubled one becomes.

Reality came to the rescue. Prophet Jeremiah's namesake appeared in the scene, stirring things up in the seminary as he was doing in the academes of Manila's Catholic elite. *Jerry* was a former dean of Ateneo de Manila's Law School, but more importantly, president of the Free Farmers' Federation. *Jerry* was a big name among Catholic college students. He was a popular speaker in Catholic campuses. A big-time Catholic layman and Jesuit-trained intellectual, he was acceptable to the young college students of Manila's elite Catholic schools. His well-reasoned advocacy for the country's rural poor resonated well with the idealistic students; among them, it became fashionable to quote his speeches and his writings, much like the way the secular college students of the day were quoting Chairman Mao's ideas. In a real way, he instigated the reformation of the Catholic Church in the Philippines. I was part of that reformation.

Our paths crossed inevitably. He became a mentor to me. I wrote my philosophy thesis on him as a developing philosopher. Through Jerry I found my bearings. I found the goal I would tie my life to. I started to re-think my career path. I found the cause I could commit to with my whole being. My vision and my mission came together: I realized *I was called to serve the poor; it did not matter whether as a priest or not.* At last, I had found my elusive niche in this world.

That was the beginning of the unraveling of my journey to the priesthood. I began to understand that it was more important to serve the poor than to become a priest. I could not become a priest of the ritual type; it would destroy me, because I never believed in platitudes. I wanted to serve the poor, as a priest if possible. I would risk losing the priesthood if the only way I could be a priest was not to serve the poor. I was again full of fervor in my vocation, although my own view of that vocation was much more defined and very specific. I was sure there would be much opposition because my own view was shared by only a few at that time. But I trusted my good sense, and I felt I was not wrong. In my reckless obstinacy, I alienated many of my peers and my superiors, but I could not care less. In time, I was targeted and ostracized, deemed unworthy to be with them any longer, and finally expelled from the seminary. In their view, I was an extremist, bad influence for the rest.

It was a big letdown for my family. My father who initially opposed my entering the seminary had already grown to like the idea of having a son-priest. My mother must have been devastated because having a son-priest was her cherished dream.

I have a family of five now. I am past my middle age. I have two sons in the best colleges in the United States and a teenage daughter struggling with her hormones and her schoolwork to make sense of her life. As I write this, my wife is dying of breast cancer. We live comfortably, by my standard, even though our house is a mobile home.

I have not led any revolutions for the poor. I am a union steward in my workplace where I do organizing work in my workplace for our union as well as represent members who have the misfortune of working under stressful conditions. I still believe in the ideas of my youth. I can look back at some twenty years in Jakarta when I experimented putting those ideas to work at my workplace, even as a business manager.

I have fought the system, undaunted by its self-serving rules, unabsorbed by the greed and selfishness that eat people alive. I have no feelings of regret. I am happy with myself. I do not look back, wishing I had done things differently. I like what I did. I take pride in what happened to me. All the difficulties and blessings in my life came to me because I made a fateful decision that changed my life forever.

Chapter 4

Why I Wanted to Become a Catholic Priest

I grew up in a small town on the eastern coast of the island of Leyte, which is on the eastern side of the Visayas, the geographically middle grouping of Philippine islands. The town is some fifteen kilometers south of the beach where General Douglas McArthur made his historic landing in October 1945 to fulfill his promised return to the Philippines and take it back from the Japanese invaders.

Our town's name, Tanauan, was derived from its function in the past. It served as the lookout place where the town's guardsmen would patiently watch out for marauding pirates from Mindanao, the southern Philippine islands, sounding the alarm when the pirates did come. Like the neighboring towns, Tanauan's population was staunchly Catholic, with the massive concrete Catholic edifice at the northern part of the *poblacion* looming large as the bastion of the people's faith.

As a young boy in a small town, I soon realized that the parish priest was in fact more important than the mayor in the life of the townspeople. Much of the life of the people revolved around religious practices.

For many families, Sunday meant choosing whether to attend the six o'clock, the eight o'clock, the ten o'clock or the five o'clock mass, as everybody was expected to go to church.

The biggest day of the year was August 15, the day of the *town fiesta*, when every family celebrated the Virgin Mary's assumption into heaven by preparing sumptuous feasts for relatives and friends from other places.

Christmas was not only Jesus' birthday but also a special day for children when they would visit the homes of their godfathers and godmothers to get their Christmas presents. It was also the season to form caroling groups and serenade families in their houses with Christmas songs, getting candies and other foodstuff in return. New Year was another religious festive occasion, celebrated by gathering the extended family together for a hearty meal at midnight after the customary family prayers.

Holy week was yet another religious occasion that would usher in four days of solemn rituals, starting with Holy Thursday's washing of the feet and culminating with the clanging of the bells on the midnight between Holy Saturday and Easter Sunday to signal Christ's resurrection.

The first Friday of each month was Sacred Heart of Jesus day when the more devout members of the church community would receive communion, preceded by a busy Thursday afternoon when people would stand in line for hours to wait for their turn at confession. Male teenagers had their own religious organization, called the Nocturnal Adorers, who would take turns in guarding the *blessed sacrament* throughout Thursday night going into first Friday morning, spending a *holy hour* in prayer.

The church's influence extended even to local sports; the town's assistant parish priest organized the summer basketball tournaments that the young men eagerly looked forward to.

It was no surprise then that kids would consider the town's priests their role models, especially as the priests were generally young and energetic. The priests ranked higher than the doctors, engineers, lawyers and teachers that the town's young kids admired.

Recruiters from the seminaries were aware of this. They targeted the best boys from the classes of graduating grade six students. It was not uncommon for a graduating class of fifty to yield as many as three recruits to the seminaries. In my older sister's class, three entered the seminary. In my older brother's class, two did. In my younger brother's class, three did. In my class, three did. Our town was such a fertile ground for the priestly vocation. In the family of my first-degree cousins, all six boys entered the seminary. In our own family, two of us did. Even a family who had only one son willingly gave him up to the seminary. To have a son studying in the seminary was very prestigious for the families in our town.

I myself was attracted by the can-do attitude of the priests in our town. I always considered myself a special person whose destiny was to do something really significant for humankind. As a young child, I was convinced that I could realize that only by becoming a priest. My father was against the idea as he was concerned the family could not afford the expenses. My mother was totally for it. Seminary officials were so intent in getting me that they offered us a sixty percent subsidy of the tuition. Even with that, my father would not budge. So, I missed the seminary for a year.

Before the start of my second year in high school, my father got a higher-paying job that took him to Guam. That made it easier for us to convince him to let me go, and he finally relented. I entered the seminary in second year high school as a *special class* student, taking special classes in Latin to make up for the year of Latin that I had missed. At the end of that year, I was at the top of the regular second year class, much to everybody's surprise. That was how I first came into notice.

I stayed in the seminary for ten years. I went in as a very young impressionable boy and came out as a determined young adult with clear ideas of what I wanted to be. The seminary certainly had a lasting influence on the values I internalized, even though these were the very same values that would place me in direct collision with my seminary superiors.

I gradually discovered in the seminary that *my early concept of the priesthood was totally flawed,* that my being in the seminary was more a search for my place in the sun which I thought I rightfully deserved as a talented person, yet contrary to the values of the person I had vowed to follow. Early on, I had committed myself to the pursuit of the top place, always. I was disciplined and single-minded in my pursuit. I reckoned that anywhere the best place is reserved for the top man, the one who excels and stands an inch or two higher in achievement over the rest.

That was before I met Jerry., the lawyer who was leading a crusade of farmers. I read his book titled *Ours To Share.* There were ideas in the book that stirred me because they seemed so right. Here was a decent man, I thought.

It seemed so natural to me that when I had to make my master's thesis in Philosophy, I chose Jerry and his budding philosophizing as my topic. I titled my thesis *A Philosopher Developing.* At the time I was thinking of making him the subject of my thesis, I had not yet met Jerry in person. I talked to a friend who was working at Jerry's office to broach to Jerry my idea. Word came back that the project was acceptable to him. I conducted my interviews in his house, and he even provided me with clippings of columns he had written for newspapers over the years.

For a year, I was totally engrossed in creating a cohesive presentation of Jerry's *Ours To Share* Philosophy. And as I studied his ideas, they started to shape my view of things.

Even before I personally met Jerry, I had joined a small group in the seminary that was actively involved in social action work. The work consisted simply of mingling with farmers, talking to them, asking them about their problems, at times explaining the country's Land Reform Code, which provided farmers some rights. It was not really much if one views it from the practical point of view of really benefiting my farmer friends. But my farmer friends seemed to enjoy the company of the bright and articulate young men who wanted to spend a lot of their spare time with farmers.

The curious thing about the whole thing was that the farmers who lived around the seminary grounds in Tagaytay, a city some fifty kilometers south of Manila in the cool highlands of Cavite province were not even Catholics. They were Protestants, but it was always understood that we were not even attempting to convert them because we never talked of religion. *We exclusively talked of things other than religion.* They called us *frater,* the Latin word for brother which was our official title in the seminary, and that was the only thing that indicated they knew who we were.

We would visit them in their houses at night when everybody else in the seminary was in his cozy room. We would go from house to house, visiting as many as four houses a night, drinking too many cups of home-brewed coffee, as we were unable to say no to their offers of coffee for fear of offending them.

My sessions with Jerry and my farmer friends started to open my eyes to what I really wanted to do. I gradually understood that my calling was to serve, not just anybody but the poorest of the poor. I also understood that the message I had to deliver for the one I had vowed to follow was not to be delivered through my mouth, as they would just be empty words. I would have to live them, and through my life and my actions, I would do my preaching. It was a revelation that liberated me.

I was tired and bored of the endless and increasingly meaningless rituals that we had to subject ourselves to. I could not imagine that I would spend the rest of my life performing those rituals day in and day out, knowing that, at some point in time, the churchgoers would open their eyes and see how inane and irrelevant our religion had become. I started to dislike the concept of God who seemed selfish, who wanted everything for Himself like the spoiled kings of the past. I could not reconcile that selfish God with the man he sent who was completely selfless. *I wanted to be a priest that mattered*, and in the context of the situation I was in, it meant I could only be an activist priest. I wanted no less.

Perhaps I was born ahead of my opportune time, *my kairos*. I was not worthy of what I wanted to be, and I did not want what I thought was not worthy of me.

I was a young man then, brash and volatile, with so many rough edges sticking out conspicuously. But the immanent force within me that transforms was strong and powerful and uncompromising. I became an anomaly to the sensibilities of the people who had the power to make the decisions that would alter the direction of my life. And so I was made to leave the seminary, forever.

I have often wondered what it all meant. Did I make a mistake? Was I too stubborn and uncompromising? Would I have done more harm if I had become an activist priest, as I had wanted to be?

I always tell my friends that the reason I have made decisions that have caused me innumerable troubles in my life journey is that I like facing myself in the mirror. I would not be able to do it and smile without making the decisions I made because I would not like what I would see there.

CHAPTER 5

TAGAYTAY AND SOCIAL WORK

O verlooking the breathtaking view of Taal volcano, Tagaytay is a small scenic city in the highlands of Cavite, a province located in the middle of the Philippines' northern island Luzon. At the time I lived there, the city was sparsely populated, totally rural in character. It had four notable places, each of which was independent of the other three and geographically stood by itself: City Hall, Taal Vista Lodge, the public market, and the Divine Word Seminary.

In the late 1960s when I was a seminarian residing at the Divine Word Seminary, the city was notorious for being warlord country dominated by two warring gangs. The mayor's older brother headed one gang while the mayor's brother-in-law headed the other. The mayor himself was aligned with his older brother who controlled the area near the public market, located at the east side. The other gang, led by his brother-in-law, controlled the area around City Hall, located at the west side, as well as the area surrounding the seminary, located at the

35

north side. The west-and-north-side gang controlled illegal gambling in the city, a lucrative source of money that the local commander of the Philippine Constabulary was probably aware of but tolerated anyway.

The gangs operated like the organized crime syndicates in the big cities of America. Every establishment in the city paid some form of tribute to the area warlord. When the seminary's shuttle-and-utility jeepney was stolen in 1969, a seminarian had to plead our case to the local boss. We waited two months before a group of unidentified men unceremoniously dumped the body of our jeepney, multicolored and all but without wheels and engine, at the entrance of the seminary chapel in the middle of the night. It stayed there for three months, a sorry reminder of our lack of real influence in the vicinity's temporal affairs.

On election days when, dressed in our flowing white cassocks, we seminarians volunteered to guard the voting precincts, we could only watch in fear and disbelief at unabashed cheating as under-age children, in the company of grim-faced men armed with M-16s, voted in lieu of their elders who could not read or write. In the afternoons after the voting, the same armed men "guarded" the canvass of the votes, as local election officials, as pre-instructed, proceeded to "read" the ballots without looking at them; as a result, only one set of candidates, those favored by the local toughie, got all the votes in the precinct. Before our first experience of Tagaytay-style elections, most of us naively believed that the sight of our white cassocks would somehow deter the cheaters from doing their usual dishonest activities. Well, things did not work out the way we expected. We ended up being the ones embarrassed, as we were too terrified to do anything.

I started living in Tagaytay in 1967, during the first year of my novitiate. Novitiate was after second-year college, when we had to suspend all academic studies for a year to concentrate on purely spiritual pursuits. As a first year novice, I was expected to spend most of my waking hours in silence, just praying and working. In Latin, it was called *Ora et Labora*.

Life in the novitiate was at once rigorous and nerve-wracking, stretching the novice's being to its psychological limits.

A regular day would start with a wake-up call at five in the morning. I would wash my face in cold water, brush my teeth, and don my cassock in time for the five-fifteen morning prayers down at the main chapel. Morning prayers would take fifteen minutes, followed by thirty minutes of meditation. Most of us would be expected to meditate in the kneeling position inside the main chapel. Mass would follow at six, usually lasting until seven.

Breakfast was at seven in a stand-alone one-story building that served as the dining place. The dining place was divided into two halls, the smaller one for the novices while the bigger one was for the major seminarians, those taking up philosophy and theology studies.

We novices would eat breakfast in silence most of the time, but once in a while, the master of novices would blurt out, "Praised be Jesus Christ!" that signaled we could break our silence after heartily responding, "Now and forever, Amen!"

After breakfast, we would go back to our dormitories to change from our cassocks to working clothes, all the while keeping silence. At seven thirty we would be at our assigned manual work posts, either at the laundry room washing clothes or outside in the fields taking out weeds while somebody read some religious book loudly. The book could be The Bible, a Vatican II documents compilation, Thomas Merton's Imitation of Christ, or some weird religious book written for contemplative monks in the middle ages.

After two hours of manual work, it was snack time at the seminary canteen, with coffee and cream and homemade bread, still keeping silence.

After snacks, we would hit the showers and don our white cassocks in time for our morning spiritual conference with the master of novices. A spiritual conference consisted of the master of novices reading a religious book while we sat silently at our desks listening to the reading. This would go on for some two hours after which we would troop down again to the dining hall for lunch.

We would eat lunch, again in silence, except when the master of novices would decide to break silence by blurting out the magic words, "Praised be Jesus Christ!", to which we would gladly shout our magic response, "Now and forever, Amen!"

After lunch, we were free to do anything except break silence until one when we were expected to be in our beds for siesta or the customary afternoon nap. Siesta would last an hour, the end of which would be signaled by a ringing bell, and we would again wash our faces and brush teeth in time for our afternoon spiritual conference.

The afternoon spiritual conference would last until four when we would finally have our first official break in silence for an hour. This was the time when we could play sports until fifteen minutes to five, at which time we would then take a shower in time for the study period at five.

We were expected to spend the next two hours silently reading religious books, including the Bible.

Dinner was at seven; this time we were free to converse with table mates. After dinner, we were free to do anything until eight thirty or nine when we would troop down again to the seminary chapel for the evening prayers. Nine thirty was lights off at the dormitories.

It was during the first year of our novitiate that we underwent the most rigorous testing in our training. We went through two ten-day retreats and one thirty-day retreat. The ten-day retreats consisted of ten consecutive days when novices would be completely silent through the day. The thirty-day retreat, considered the most difficult hurdle, consisted of three consecutive ten-day retreats with one free day in-between the ten-day silent days. As far as I can remember, there would always be at least one in a class who would have a nervous breakdown, and our class of forty-four was no exception.

It was during those trying days that I learned to converse with myself, what with all those ideas racing around in my head with no other person to discuss them with. I learned to listen to myself, even argue with myself, in the deafening silence of my solitude. I was in the midst of forty-three other people, and yet I felt so alone, like I was in some strange foreign country with no one to talk to but myself. We did not even dare to look at each other's eyes for fear that we would be conversing with each other through our minds. We were all brought to the brink of madness.

The first ten-day retreat was done just before we had our investiture for the novitiate. The investiture was the ritual when we first donned our white cassocks. That was our transition from the minors to the majors. The thirty-day retreat was conducted sometime in the middle of that first novitiate year. The second ten-day retreat was at the end of the first novitiate year.

During the second novitiate year, we resumed our formal schooling by starting to take philosophy subjects. Comparatively, that would be third-year college, with a major in philosophy. All the philosophy subjects required for a bachelor's degree in philosophy were crammed into two years, and the first of those years was our second novitiate year. We were still under the guidance of the novice master, but we were practically major seminarians because of our philosophy studies.

For two of my classmates and me, that year also marked our introduction to social work among farmers. The seminary's social action group formally invited us to train with them; they even secured the permission of the novice master so that we could be given some leeway to attend their activities. We were of course just too happy to be in an "action" group, but looking at it from hindsight now, the process of selecting us to join the group smacked of elitism. The group of upper class seminarians had chosen the three top academic achievers in our class to join them, implying that the rest of the class did not make the grade to be social worker trainees because they were not smart enough.

That consciousness was farthest from our mind at the time as we were excited about the prospect of being able to do something that had immediate impact and not merely preparatory, which was basically our view of the 14-year grind to become priests. There was a world out there that we were missing even as we struggled to overcome the tedium of living isolated from the real world. Social work gave us a pretext to get a glimpse of what we would face later as priests.

The seminary's social action group members were working closely with an organization of farmers headed by Jerry Montemayor.

As a member of the seminary's social action group, I was expected to work closely with Montemayor's organization. This gave me the chance to travel to Central Luzon to attend teach-ins, meetings, workshops, conventions, and seminars of farmers. I also met like-minded young students and professionals who were working with the farmers. I felt no longer isolated and bored. I was at last connected to a network of people who cared about real things and real problems.

My base was the city of Tagaytay. My special friends were the little people around the seminary campus, the farmers who tilled the hilly fields of Tagaytay. *Mag-asawang Ilat* (Lover Rivers) was the name of the village just across from the seminary that was my usual destination for my nocturnal escapades. My good friend *Mang Entin* was my constant companion and guide. The village became my village, and the village people became my people. I did not do anything tangible for them, but as I began to know them by their names, in my heart they became my closest friends.

During summer, members of the social action group would be encouraged to join summer camps, our version of summer camps. On two successive summers, I spent the major part of my summer vacation in the barrios of Tarlac, known then for home-grown communist insurgencies. During the first summer, I was a member of a team of six that spent six weeks in the barrio of *Talimundok* in the town of Concepcion, Ninoy Aquino's hometown. The next summer, I went with another team of six to live in a barrio in the city of Tarlac. In both cases, we did not really do anything except live and mingle with the farmer-residents there. It was a way of re-educating us young people then who had spent most of our lives in urban areas among the more affluent sectors of society. Of course, we would get to know first-hand the problems of the farmers, especially those relating to their status as tenants of lands they tilled but did not own.

In my mind, Tagaytay would always be my home even though I lived there for only four years. I discovered my true self there; it will always be the place of my re-birth

CHAPTER 6

WHY I WROTE THIS PIECE

I had just undergone a double bypass heart surgery the day before. It was Sunday morning, and only a young Malaysian resident doctor was around at the hospital. Both the thoracic surgeon who had conducted the operation and the chief of the ICU were at home with their families. A major complication occurred that day after my surgery.

While still in the ICU room, I had difficulty breathing. My oxygen intake was only 40%, and I was in great discomfort. The resident physician's diagnosis was that water had filled my lungs. A minor surgery was needed to relieve it.

I was losing hope fast. I felt I was just minutes away from total darkness. I felt like giving up was easier than holding on to dear life. I could not hold on much longer. I closed my eyes, clasped the hand of the nurse on my right, and started counting mentally. *This was it!* The nurses were frantically trying to contact the chief surgeon who had operated on me. Finally they got him on the phone, but he told them it would take him some twenty minutes to reach the hospital. As I lay there gasping for breath, I thought it would take him too long to be of real help.

Taking stock of the situation, the Malaysian doctor finally decided he would do the minor operation. Over the phone, he assured the chief surgeon that he had done it once, and the patient had lived. The last thing I saw before passing out was his stoic face peering down at me through eye-glassed eyes. I lived through that ordeal to tell this story.

The next day, as I went to the toilet to pass water, I stared at the tiled wall, as I stood in front of the toilet bowl unable to do it. I waited several minutes but couldn't will the water out. The anesthesia used during the operation had probably numbed my body too much that I had temporarily lost control of my bladder. So, the nurses attached me to a catheter, at the end of which was a plastic gallon to collect my urine. From then on, for some six days I had to carry the container wherever I went.

That was not the end of my ordeal. For several days after that I could not move my bowels. At first, I was more annoyed than alarmed. On the fourth day, however, my skin started turning yellow. This went on for another three days at which time everybody was alarmed. The chief surgeon, who was still acting as my main doctor, suggested that a liver specialist examine me. When the specialist finished with his examinations, he declared that it was the antibiotic that they gave me during the operation that had triggered what appeared to be an allergic reaction. He told me to drink more fluids, and that I did. Initially, my urine came out dark brown even as I passed large amounts of it into the plastic gallon for several days. The color turned lighter with each passing day until it became light, clear yellow. By then, my liver condition had improved.

It was on one night during that difficult period that I started pondering about my life. I did a recap of my life up to that point. I asked myself what I had achieved with my life until then.

The musings of a man who thinks he is dying has a way of revising the order of priorities of the various elements in his life-view. As some hitherto-important features blur from view, the really important come into sharp focus. I started to see things from a new perspective, experiencing a reincarnation of some sort, an *epiphany*, having a more profound understanding of the world around me.

I realized then that when one looks at the past from the end-point, a lot of things look different. I saw that the things that I exerted so much effort on were those that had actually very little significance when viewed from the end-point. I felt so foolish and stupid. I saw very clearly the missed opportunities in my life, and there were quite many of those. I also recognized the seemingly trite things that I had done that actually loom large and significant when seen from the end-point; those were the little kindnesses that I had occasionally permitted myself to dispense.

The enemies that I hated so much for inflicting deep emotional wounds on my psyche (that I had always carried around just beneath my consciousness) became insignificant and unimportant. They were not worth the effort and time I devoted to thinking about them. All the anger and hate that I carried around did not really matter in the end. They only made me bitter beneath the surface as I went through life, haunting my dreams, making me thirsty for revenge in some undefined way. I looked back and understood that I had become a less pleasant man because I had let these feelings clasp me in their subtle hands.

What gripped me most was the realization that I had wasted time on the inconsequential. Life is too precious to be spent brooding and hating. I appreciated the occasional niceties I had shown other people because in the end these were the things that really matter. I wished I had more of those to show at the end-point.

One of the things that I felt then was an intense sense of lack of accomplishment. I felt I had not done enough, that I could have done so much more, that even if I live some more the remaining period would be so much shorter than the wasted period. I saw time ahead as more precious because of its brevity. Every little time available had to be used wisely. Time ahead was seen as overtime in much in the same way as in basketball or football, a short extension within which one has to score as many points as one can.

I was given a gift. My time was extended. I do not know for how long, but I know it will be much shorter than the 55 years I have already spent. How many people have been blessed to see their life from the end-point and then given a life extension? I occasionally shed tears, whether for joy or sadness is really irrelevant, when I feel the surge that comes from the realization that I can see things from a new perspective, having the rare wisdom of viewing reality in a new way, and really seeing the gradations of the different colors within that reality because I have seen it from the end-point.

I can understand why Mattie Stepanek, the small chronically sick boy who wrote poems of hope, had such a rosy view of things. He understood that he had such a short life expectation that it would be great waste to be sad.

CHAPTER 7

BADGES OF HONOR

We like to wear badges of honor because they show to the people who see them that we have done something of great value that deserves public admiration. Of course, we are proud to be associated with whatever lofty principles those badges represent.

Well, I have been wearing badges of honor for some time now. People do not see them because they are not on my outer garments. They are invisible to human eyes because I wear them deep--in my heart of hearts, in my memory. They constantly remind me of the values and principles I have lived for.

I am writing about them now, still in the privacy of my private essays, to show to the people around me, especially the people who are dear to me, to whom I will bequeath these essays, when I got them and for what I got them. Hopefully, they will help explain what I had stood for and what I was trying to accomplish.

I received my first badge of honor at the end of my high school years. I am a very competitive person who fights tooth and nails to be at the top of any academic competition. During my fourth year in high school I was determined to beat everybody in my class academically and succeeded. I had a grade point average (GPA) of 93.5% while my nearest rival had a 90.5% GPA. When the graduation honors were announced, however, I learned that somebody with a GPA of 89% was declared valedictorian, and I was relegated to first honorable mention, third in rank. Two of my teachers, who attended the meeting to determine the graduating class rankings and were sympathetic, explained to me that the priest who was the academic affairs head had made all decisions regarding the rankings. There were no satisfactory or logical explanations as to why I did not get the highest ranking. My mother was so dejected that she refused to attend my graduation. She wrote the priest who was our prefect of discipline (different from the academic affairs priest) about her disappointment. He answered her by pointing out that I had entered the seminary to become a priest, not to seek earthly awards, and that this injustice should be seen as a test of my resolve to strive for higher things. I swallowed my pride, steeled myself throughout my lonely graduation experience, and reluctantly gave up what I believed was mine by merit. That was how I gave myself my first badge of honor. Nobody remembers what happened that day except me. The two other people who knew were my mother and my best friend who are both dead now.

Perhaps you the reader wonder what was it that I gave myself and how did I give it to myself. I did not give myself a physical badge. I gave myself a mental badge, a promise that I will not forget what I gave up that day for the sake of my vocation, the priesthood. God was my witness, but if it turned out that there is no God, then I will be the witness to my own sacrifice. Does it really matter that somebody stole what I had earned? If there is a God and there is ultimate judgment, then all the earthly pleasures do not matter, and all the badges of honor that we mentally wear are justified and have meaning not only to ourselves.

I received my second badge of honor when I was expelled from the seminary. I was declared unworthy to become a priest and banished forever from the one thing that I had dedicated ten years of my life in preparation and for which I had renounced everything I ever desired. This did not come as a complete surprise to me. A few months earlier, several of my classmates had voted me out in our annual cleansing of the rolls. The rule for voting out a colleague stipulated that the person voting out a colleague had to provide a grave reason for his recommendation. Although the voting itself was done anonymously, the reasons were copied into a piece of paper and given to the person being voted out. That was how I learned about the accusations that my colleagues leveled at me. But those accusations were not the reasons for my ouster. The real reason for voting me out was that there were a quite a lot of my colleagues who hated me specifically for ruining the seminary's family feast that year because of what they considered my disruptive behavior. The seminary's family feast was celebrated annually with a program, games, and special food. That year, we were celebrating it while the whole country was in the middle of crippling strikes by workers and public transportation drivers in protest of gas price increases. A group of us wanted to bring that reality into our celebration through a mock protest, and by acclamation, I was designated as the spokesman of the group. It was intended as a dig at our insensitivity in the midst of a national crisis, but it backfired, as the audience became genuinely angry at our mock protest. Our small group became a pariah during the whole celebration, and I was marked for eventual crucifixion. When I did read that piece of paper, the vehemence of the accusations surprised me, especially because the most serious ones were false. My colleagues wanted to crucify me, even if they had to lie to accomplish it. It was a most disappointing experience for me, as I imagined my accusers gloating at *getting their pound of flesh*. I wondered what kind of priests these men *with little vicious hearts* would turn out to be. As far as the administrators of the seminary were concerned, I was guilty until I could prove myself innocent. In their view, it was preposterous to even imagine that my accusers were lying. So I was doomed. When the final decision from Rome came, I took it like a soldier being sentenced in his court martial. I packed my things and headed for home. But in my heart of hearts, I knew that I had been falsely accused, and I deserved my second mental badge of honor. I knew that everybody, as usual, would forget his part in the sordid affair, but I, the victim, was determined not to forget.

I received my third badge of honor a year later after teaching for a year in a college run by Catholic nuns. I had taught Logic to college girls in that Catholic school and had received superior ratings for teaching competence from the students. I was confident that I had found my place in the academe as a conscientious and competent teacher. I enjoyed what I was doing. But that was also the time when Marcos' government was watching closely the activities of students and teachers in the campuses. School officials were quite jittery about possible reprisals from the government for anti-government activities of their students and faculty members. Towards the end of that school year, the nun who was the vice president for academic affairs called me to her office to inform me that the school was releasing me the next school year as I was an excess teacher. There was something in the way she said it that told me she was lying. I was later able to confirm that because the next school year they hired an ex-seminarian, who had just left the seminary and was an acquaintance of mine, to teach the subjects I had been teaching.

Moreover, I later found out that the rector of the seminary, who was a former teacher of mine in the seminary and with whom I had verbal clashes in the past when I was president of our class, was a friend of the school directress. It was quite easy to add up the pieces and come to the conclusion that they conspired to terminate my services for reasons other than my teaching competence. I knew that within a week those people would forget their parts in that termination after savoring that one instance of playing all-powerful, but I was determined not to forget. It was another mental badge of honor that would keep reminding me who I was and what I stood for. I was the victim, but the injustice did not make me hateful or vindictive. I constantly reminded myself that if and when I had the power, I would act differently.

I received my fourth badge of honor six months later after teaching in another Catholic school run by nuns. As in the previous year, I received superior ratings from the students for competence in teaching. I taught Philosophy of Religion that year. That was the year when the intelligence agents of Marcos' government threatened to crack down on activists in the campuses. By that time, my activist years were over. I was just lying low, chastened by the disappointing events of the previous years. I was, however, friendly with some of the activist figures in the campus, which proved to be my undoing. As I was preparing for the second semester, I was called into the office of the nun who was the academic directress of the college and told quite casually not to expect any load in the second semester. She explained to me that she could not vouch for me to the government authorities, as she did not know me that well. She was therefore releasing me from my teaching position. I went home and cried.

That was how I finally realized that in the real world, people with authority often wield it so lightly and so irresponsibly. Somehow the notion that people with authority must ultimately be accountable for every exercise of that authority grew on me. I always tell people that that is the reason I believe there is a God. If there were no God, *I would have to invent him to give meaning to my badges of honor.*

There were subsequent badges of honor that I gave myself for the many fights I waged to remain a decent man. Those fights were not easy for me. I always paid some price; each badge was for the price I paid. I fought for principles because I wanted to be a decent man, and a decent man would have fought for them. Every badge of honor was like an elixir that made me stronger in my resolve to be a decent man.

After I die, I would like people to remember me as "the man who had no nasty bone in his body", who only wanted to do the right things. Even if there were no God, I would have been truly happy at death, knowing that I helped create a better world around me.

PART 3:
TRANSITION 1

CHAPTER 8

A LONG SHOT

I was surprised to receive a call from the executive search company in Manila that Thursday morning in May 1981. My contact at John Clements (the search company) told me to be at the Mandarin Hotel for an interview at two in the afternoon that day. On the pretext that I had a mysterious stomach ailment, at eleven in the morning I hurriedly left the office by taxi to go home and be properly dressed for the interview that would change the course of my life.

That was how I met Anak Agung, the managing director of SC Johnson Indonesia. He was in Manila that day to conduct interviews for his company.

On my way to the hotel, I was thinking I would probably be one among a hundred applicants for the marketing position that I had applied for. Three months earlier, a recruiter from John Clements had phoned to ask me if I would be interested in a marketing assignment in Indonesia. I immediately said yes, thinking it was a choice assignment, although a long shot for me. I quickly sent my resume to the executive search company and quickly forgot about it--- until I got the call that Thursday morning. My previous and current bosses at Philippine Refining Company, where I was a junior product manager of the Detergents Division, had both been previously assigned in Indonesia, and they had glowing recollections of their experiences there.

At the hotel, I went up to the room designated as the interview room, a bit surprised to notice that I was the only person waiting outside the door. A few minutes later, as the door opened, an office mate--somebody from our media section--came out. We nodded at each other, quietly acknowledging that we were competing for the same position. Then I noticed our host. A young man about as old as I was, he smiled as he greeted and asked me to come into his room.

He asked a number of difficult but provocative questions, impressing me with his intellectual acuity and sophistication. He seemed friendly and genuinely interested in my responses to his questions. The interview seemed to me like an honest conversation between two earnest professionals who just hit it off extremely well the first time around. As I was leaving, he casually asked me to come back for another session on Saturday at two in the afternoon. The invitation to return should have indicated to me a not-so-subtle interest, but I was not biting that early yet.

The next morning, I received a call from the secretary of SC Johnson's regional director informing me that the regional director--technically Anak Agung's direct superior--was expecting me for lunch that day at the hotel near his office. The call was at ten in the morning, totally unexpected. I was at the office, in T-shirt and rubber shoes, under-dressed for business lunch, as I had just finished inspecting something in the factory area. There was no time to go back home and change. I told the secretary that I was not really dressed for formal company that day, but if necessary, I would go anyway.

That was how I met Tito Adad, a Filipino of Syrian ancestry whose previous job was managing director of SC Johnson Indonesia. I would find out later that he mentored Anak Agung for the managing director job. He became regional director a few years earlier, relinquishing the managing director position to Agung.. He was an animated sort of guy, talking non-stop in a staccato but disarming manner, instantly putting me at ease over our buffet lunch.

The whole thing was beginning to intrigue me; the lunch invitation seemed to indicate that they were seriously considering me for the job. Up to that point, I had not really considered it as even remotely possible; *it was all a fishing expedition to me.* As I was leaving to go back to the office, Tito informed me that Anak Agung was expecting me for another round of interview in his hotel room, on Sunday rather than on Saturday. I mentally tried to tell myself that there were probably five of us candidates competing for the job, that I was still a long shot for it, but I could not help feeling a certain thrill for being considered a serious contender.

That Sunday afternoon, I went back to Anak Agung's room, expecting to be brought back to earth. It did not happen, as after a few innocuous questions, he made a very specific proposal. He invited me to work for him at SC Johnson Indonesia in Jakarta, declaring that they would start working on the required documents immediately. I sealed my fate when I said yes, not really knowing what I had gotten myself into. Various thoughts were racing simultaneously through my head as I headed home, trying to sort out the many things I had to do in the next few weeks.

I talked to my girlfriend Del about getting married before departing for Indonesia. It was all so sudden, but I succeeded in persuading her into agreeing to a simple wedding, with only our immediate families attending. Her mother was not really pleased, but she tried to hide her displeasure, although I could sense it anyway.

My mother was in California at the time, having joined my older brother as an immigrant. She tried to bargain for a postponement of our wedding. I told her it was okay if she could not come home to attend, as we really did not need her for that. I did not mean it to sound so brutal. She was furious, of course, and my eldest sister, who was visiting her in the United States from Nigeria, wrote me an emotionally charged letter that conveyed how bitter they felt about my telling my mother we did not need her. My mother came home anyway with my second eldest sister, who had joined them in the United States, to attend my wedding.

The whole wedding thing cost us four thousand pesos, the equivalent of two hundred dollars, *cheap for such an occasion*. That covered the cost of my suit and pants, Del's wedding dress, the wedding rings that Del's friend made for us, and the food we ate at Kowloon Restaurant. Del's boss Ernie and best friend Josie were the principal sponsors while my closest office mate-friend Gert was the wedding car driver (and car owner). Ernie gave us our two-day stay at a five-star hotel after the wedding as his gift. My very close friend from our seminary days, Caloy Rodriguez, was the officiating priest, refusing to accept anything for his services. During the two weeks between our wedding and my departure for Jakarta, we temporarily stayed at a pension house along Calamba Street in Sampaloc, Manila, near the western border of Quezon City.

Although the flight from Manila to Jakarta was itself uneventful, internally I experienced interestingly complex emotions--a mixture of thrill and worry. I was not sure what I had gotten myself into, and predictably I was apprehensive about my adventure into the unknown. I felt lonely because my new bride was not with me and would be joining me only after several months. On the other hand, I was glad that I was finally leaving the Philippines. I could not stand anymore the repressive Marcos regime that stifled free speech and dissent. I was also dissatisfied with the company where I had been working because top management put more importance on how people dressed than how they actually performed work. I needed a new environment where my skills would be better appreciated without sucking up to top management. Indonesia promised to be the place for my professional rebirth.

Indonesia proved to be the new frontier I had imagined it would be. I spent 18 satisfying years there. I built my professional reputation there, successfully steering two companies to business success. I made a small fortune there, with the regular savings we made from my expatriate pay. I raised a happy family of five there, replete with the uncommon luxury of having three maids and two drivers around us to tend to our needs. I developed and honed my professional skills to the fullest there, learning to take business risks and win as well as to develop fine and skillful subordinates. I flourished into the successful top business manager that I had always believed I was capable of becoming, without engaging in the distracting game of office politics.

PART 4: FAMILY

CHAPTER 9

LIFEMATE

Two and a half months ago, my siblings surprised me by arranging my renewal of marriage vows with my wife. To catch us unprepared, they set it a day earlier than our actual 25th wedding anniversary. Everything was kept hush-hush up to the last minute, with the connivance of our children. They sprang it on us after I came home from work. They even bought a wedding gown for my wife. I was totally unprepared for it that I had to wear my unwashed Barong Tagalog (a traditional formal attire for Filipino men) that I last wore for my older brother's funeral a year earlier.

The high point of the occasion was our renewal of vows. As we read the words that would re-commit us to each other for the rest of our married life, Del and I broke down in tears. My wife Del has 4th stage breast cancer, diagnosed a year earlier at about the same time my older brother died from drowning. We know the days of our marriage are numbered. We have both been in a state of denial, pushing back in our minds what we know is inevitable. The occasion painfully brought it to the foreground.

I met Del while I was studying for a doctorate in philosophy at the University of Santo Tomas in Manila. I was twenty-five years old then, having received my master's degree in philosophy eight months earlier. I had enrolled in the Educational Psychology class of Dr. Dolly Garcia. Educational Psychology was a cognate subject for me, meaning, although it was not a philosophy subject, I could use the units earned as elective units for my doctoral degree in Philosophy.

Del was taking the subject as a requirement for her master's degree in sociology. She was twenty-two years old then, working at the University of Santo Tomas both as faculty member of the sociology department and as assistant director of the social research center of the university.

The first day of that class was typical, with formal introductions both by the teacher and the individual students. Informal introductions followed during the break. That was the opportunity to sort out the people around you, meaning, those sitting in front and behind you, as well as on your sides. Del was sitting behind me to my right, unobtrusive but looking approachable and friendly. I remember turning around and asking for her name, to which she answered softly, with an almost inaudible voice, Del. It was an almost forgettable introduction, civil and ordinary.

As a student, I always participate actively in class discussions, and this class was no exception. During one of our earlier sessions, I had just finished expressing my opinion about an issue when a lady sitting in front of me raised her hand and forcefully expressed a contrary opinion on the same issue. I was piqued by the idea that another person in class would dare to contradict me in a class discussion, something that I was not used to in my undergraduate courses. I soon learned that the soft-spoken classmate who used to sit behind me but was now sitting in front was just as opinionated as I was on a lot of issues.

It would have ended as a curiosity item except for a chance meeting at the school canteen one evening before the start of class. Casual greetings led to a friendly conversation at a canteen table over snacks and soft drinks. I found her quite engaging and a very interesting conversation partner. We found so many topics to talk about during that one fateful occasion. That chance conversation led to many eagerly anticipated conversations. From that evening on, I made it a point to be at the canteen at least half an hour before class in anticipation of another enjoyable conversation with her.

To continue with our conversations, I sat beside her in class. Several of our classmates started noticing how we seemed to enjoy communicating in short inaudible whispers during class, even as we participated in class discussions. I truly enjoyed her company, and our conversations were always about some interesting topic, like politics, movies, even philosophy. Her ideas were always well thought out, revealing an uncanny, earthy wisdom that fascinated me no end. I considered our conversations as intellectual adventures where we could give free rein to our free spirits and imagination.

Del and I became very close friends. We would set dates on weekends so that we could continue with our interrupted conversations. We spent hours and hours talking about so many interesting things. What developed was a relaxed relationship, without the awkward feeling that we were involved in some romantic relationship.

I knew something was happening to me when I started missing her whenever she was not with me. I was not sure how she regarded our friendship, but I was sure I did not want to lose her as a friend, something that had happened to me a few years earlier because I was foolish enough to try to bring an enjoyable friendship to a qualitatively higher level.

My curiosity got the better of me, so I asked her to go with me to Tagaytay on a weekend to visit my alma mater for a day. We spent the day there at the Divine Word Seminary campus talking about a lot of things, but all that time, we were both probably thinking about why we were there in the first place. As we walked the long road from the seminary to the national road, I steeled my nerve to ask the inevitable question that had been bothering me. How did she view our relationship? She was quite evasive about her answer, but I could detect a certain hesitation that kept me hoping. On the bus back to Manila, I kept telling her that what I felt for her was more than ordinary friendship, but she kept explaining it away, so we ended up telling each other that we did not want to lose each other as a friend. I was willing to leave it at that. It was Saturday.

On Monday afternoon she called me to say she wanted to see me after her class that evening. On the way to the school, I was in agony thinking that she would ask me not to see her again. I braced myself for whatever bad news I was about to hear. I must have looked deathly pale when I finally met her, like a man about to receive a death sentence. She looked at me, smiled, and said, "Yes." I looked at her, not quite sure what she meant by it. She proceeded to hold my hand, and then I was sure.

CHAPTER 10

THE FIRST BORN

Del and I were newly married when I left Manila for Jakarta, Indonesia. She followed some eight months later after tying the loose ends of her budding teaching career at the University of Santo Tomas. We were eager to start a family there in our new place, away from the influences of kin and friends. Everything seemed exciting because we knew we had a free hand to try out new things, without the encumbrance of tradition and well-meaning advice from elders.

Both of us were strong-willed individuals (we still are), and we savored our independence from convention. We were going to mold our own microcosm, our family.

It was into this haven of excited experimenters that Hamlet was born. In many senses, he was the fledgling product of our inexperienced and shaky attempts to create our brand of parenting. We did not always agree on whose ideas were better, but our efforts were always earnest, even in our frequent disagreements.

We saw ourselves as belonging to the left-leaning liberal side of the social spectrum, and we agreed to nurture a free environment in the confines of our modest home. Our children probably were not even aware how ideologically different our home environment was from our friends' and neighbors'.

Early on, we found that conscious parenting can be exciting, exhausting, and exasperating, especially when the object of our attention seemed to have an attitude all his own.

I was the one who gave our firstborn his name Hamlet. His name was actually a *statement* that only I could understand and explain. A good part of my belief system went into that name. Through that name, I wanted to say that, as my son grows up, he himself would ultimately determine what he would become. I was actually fascinated by the phrase "to be or not to be", which I took to mean that one determines one's own destiny.

I did not know it then that I, as parent, would have so much difficulty abiding by that precept with regard to his development. Even as a baby, he was already showing that he was just as strong-willed (the other descriptive word is *stubborn*) as his parents were (and still are). In the words of our close friend Perry, Hamlet was already "marching to his own drums" at the age of four.

When Hamlet's younger brother Voltaire was born, he looked so much cuter than Hamlet that everybody seemed to be naturally drawn to him. In our fear that this would generate envy from his older brother, we decided that one of us would have to compensate for that by focusing attention on Hamlet, and I volunteered to do that. That was why, during much of his early years, I was Hamlet's constant companion. I devoted all my free time to making him feel like he was my only son, the one who mattered most to me. I became his one-on-one mentor, and I tried to teach him everything I knew. ·

On Saturdays and Sundays, I brought him to all the nice places in and around Jakarta, urging him to try all kinds of things, filling him in on all the things I knew. I accompanied him to his out-of-school math, music, and swimming classes, always acting like a stage parent, making things possible for him.

Even when he was still too small to understand, I was already talking to him about basketball --- the game I loved to play --- and soccer --- the game I loved to watch and analyze. I related to him many stories about both NBA and FIFA heroes ---sports greats like Bob Cousy and Larry Bird in basketball and Diego Maradona and Marco van Basten in soccer --- and explained what made them so great. I regaled him with stories about my own exploits in academics and sports, always emphasizing that dedication and hard work were the keys to achieving full potential.

I did not know it then, but later he would tell me that he was overwhelmed by my stories about my exploits and achievements both in sports, the academe, and work. Without intending to, I created in his mind a superman that he had to match and surpass as he grew up. Instead of being an inspiration, I became a dead weight on his young shoulders. He thought I wanted him to match and surpass me. Instead of energizing him, the stories depressed him, but he kept these thoughts to himself.

These thoughts burst into the open during the tantrums of his teenage years, when he reached the age of fifteen and was straddling between a sense of inadequacy and a surge of rebellion. I did not know what to do. How could I undo things that I was not even aware of? The situation was compounded because I became aware of these his inner problems at the time when he was in high school preparing for college, when I was pushing him to do his utmost to get into the best colleges.

The confluence of pressure, anxiety, and sense of uncertainty put an unnecessary strain on him.

Towards the end of high school, he was accepted by Stanford University, a feat that was unprecedented in his school. Tennyson High School was a struggling public high school in Hayward from which less than half of the graduates continued into college. At the time of Hamlet's graduation, Hayward was at the lowest rung among cities in California in terms of educational achievement, and Tennyson was ranked lowest among the three high schools in Hayward.

He scored 1435 out of a possible 1600 in the SAT exams and. graduated valedictorian from a class of 400, but his acceptance into Stanford, announced before graduation, overshadowed all his other achievements in school. When that lone window of opportunity opened, he was there, ready to go in. I was part of that long struggle, and I remember I had tears in my eyes when we attended his one-day orientation at Stanford.

I had been egging him to apply to as many schools as possible, and make sure that six of these were the best schools in America. He had resisted me all the way although he did it grudgingly. The schools that accepted him were NYU, Boston College, UC Berkeley, UCLA, USC, Tulane University, and Miami University. He was wait-listed by Cornell University, Brown, Amherst, and Chicago University. When he received the acceptance papers from Stanford, all the others faded from view. He had gotten his first choice, beyond his wildest dreams.

All through Hamlet's high school years, I acted as his personal coach in essay writing. I corrected his essays ruthlessly, and we would go into heated discussions later about my corrections. I still felt that he was not as polished in his writing as I would have wanted him to be. He always argued that he was getting **A**s for every paper he submitted. I felt that he was not working hard enough on his academic work in preparation for college in the best schools, but he would counter that the grades he was getting attested to the hard work he was doing.

It is really sad when your words prove to be prescient because much *as you might relish saying I told you so*, the damage has been done and time past cannot be recovered. His essays in Stanford were not getting the **A**s he was used to in high school. He also found out that in Stanford even hard work without earlier stringent preparation would only earn **B**s. He did earn **A**s but only by driving himself relentlessly.

When he was at Stanford, he started asking for help again in his writing. Through his four years at Stanford, I saw a gradual maturing of his skills. I was pleasantly surprised to find in his final year his papers showing the polish that I expected his papers to have. This was my eldest son finally coming of age.

There has always been a dilemmatic tension in my relationship with Hamlet. I sometimes pushed him too hard, but I was always afraid he would break in the process. Yet, I always felt that there were opportunities that were opening up for him that his mom and I never had a chance to see in our days, opportunities that we in our days could have exploited fully. I did not want him to miss these, and he had to be ready when these came within reach. After all, he was our son, and we knew he had the genes to excel.

CHAPTER 11

POPOT

My wife Del and I waited until the intervals between her contractions had become as frequent as every twenty minutes. Based on her previous birthing experience, I thought I still had enough time to bring her to the maternity hospital that was forty minutes away from our house by car. We thought our previous experience with our first-born a year and a half earlier was sufficient guide for us about when our second baby would come out. That first time, her labor had taken thirty-six hours. That time, I was stuck in the lobby of the hospital waiting for the baby to be born, with enough time to read a novel from cover to cover. This time, I was determined to take my time, all the while thinking it would at least be two hours before childbirth. Depositing my wife at the delivery room with the nurses, I braced myself for a long wait.

A bookstore was just two blocks away from the hospital, so I decided to walk over and buy a paperback. It took fifteen minutes to do all of that. As I was coming back, a harried-looking nurse met me at the gate, instructing me to put on the green-colored sterile uniform that visitors must wear before entering the delivery room. On the way to the delivery room, she informed me that my wife had delivered our baby while I was out. I discovered later that it occurred five minutes after I left her in the delivery room. As I entered the room, my wife weakly smiled at me and told me our baby was a boy. She was a little disappointed as she expected a girl. *We were so sure it was going to be a girl.* Earlier, we had agreed that she would choose the name if the baby was a girl. Now I had the naming option, as with our first baby.

I had a favorite name in reserve, just in case. I had always used it as my pseudo pen name in my younger years when I was in the seminary. Now I was glad I could use it permanently! And that was how our second son got his name, Voltaire.

Through the years, he developed entirely different feelings for that name. In his early days in school, he detested it because nobody in Indonesia seemed to get it right. Quite often he was called Wortel, which was disconcerting to him because it means *carrot* in Indonesian. At times, people would call him Walter, which is close enough but not quite right. Later, in his high school years in America, it became his source of pride, as people complimented him about the illustrious person he was named after. It took some time but it gradually dawned on him that it was an uncommon name that carried with it a certain mystique associated with quite a controversial thinker and the renowned author of *Candide*. He started to see the logic to the naming, that he was meant to be special. His name was, after all, not that burdensome as he initially imagined, but quite challenging and unique.

My own reasons for liking and choosing the name were unique. There was a real person in the Philippines with that name, my contemporary for whom I had great admiration although we never met personally. He was a student leader at the University of the Philippines, about three years older than I was when I first heard about him. He eventually became a lawyer and a youth activist, but his life was abruptly cut short by a mysterious sickness. He was some kind of a legend in my circle of friends, and the mystique of his life and name fascinated me. In fact, I adopted him as my role model. It was more for him than for the more illustrious predecessor that I attached a certain aura of importance to the name. I started using the name as my pen name whenever I could from college onwards.

As a toddler, my firstborn could not quite pronounce his name Hamlet. He eventually ended up calling himself *Pepet* and could not be dissuaded to change to another, more audibly palatable, name. In the search for an appropriate nickname for my second born, I thought of a name that would not make my firstborn envious because it sounded better, something close to Pepet that sounded Indonesian. I eventually decided that the easiest alternative was to replace the *e* in Pepet with another vowel that would somehow still be relatable to the name Voltaire. I finally chose the vowel *o* and that was how I came up with the name Popot. From then on, it was Pepet and Popot, the inseparable brothers. When they were small, they actually liked their nicknames, but later in America when they were in their teens, they hated those nicknames because of the unsophisticated sounds and their puerile roots.

Popot was about one and half years old when my wife and I noticed a strange phenomenon about his development as a young child. There were long stretches, like three months, when he seemed to be hibernating. He would be very quiet, not saying anything, seemingly lost in his own thoughts, unaware of his surroundings. Initially, this bothered us, as it seemed like he was regressing in his mental development. After behaving this way for a long time, he would suddenly burst into frenetic activity as if he was released from being coiled up for so long. I started noticing this on Saturdays when, because I did not have to go to the office, I would stay in bed longer until late in the morning. At seven in the morning, he would start walking around, loudly talking to himself, exhibiting behavior that showed he remembered everything that had happened during the three months when he was quietly hibernating. My wife and I were initially shocked at witnessing those flashes of clarity and energy, when it seemed as if he was trying to prove to the world around him that although he had been silent, he had been observing and taking in everything all that time. Then, just as suddenly, he would crawl back into his distant shell and hibernate again.

Another incredible thing happened when he was two and a half. At that time, his older brother was already going to play school where the medium of instruction was English. Popot stayed at home with our three maids, watching television. There was only one TV station in Jakarta at that time, and in the mornings the station would show Sesame Street. Unnoticed by everybody else, the two kids started to converse in English. With Pepet, that was sort of expected, but with Popot, that was a big surprise as nobody had taken any effort to teach him English. Somehow, he learned to speak English just by watching Sesame Street and trying it out with his older brother.

Even as a very young child, Popot exhibited a mixture of boundless energy and lack of focus. He was in constant movement. He would continually hurt himself bumping into furniture. He was the typical "I jump before I think" boy. Several times he locked himself inside rooms by turning the keys that were deliberately left inside the keyholes. He was still too small to turn them back so we often had to ask our driver to climb through the window or ceiling to get at the key. It came to a point where Popot was terrified to enter rooms which were locked from the inside, knowing that he would be tempted to turn the key or lock the knob almost by reflex. He would also often wander away from us in shopping malls, only to find himself lost among the lines of merchandise, not knowing how to go back. As we frantically searched for him, we would hear from the PA system about a lost boy looking for his parents. One time, he locked himself in the mall's public toilet, and I had to calmly coach him how to unlock the doorknob while he was crying desperately from inside. Later on, we consulted a psychiatrist and learned that he had a mild case of Attention Deficit Disorder or hyperactivity.

His short attention span notwithstanding, Popot exhibited flashes of brilliance that amazed his teachers. Although he had difficulty following his teachers' instructions on how to do his school work and assignments, somehow he found his own way of arriving at the correct answers. His math teacher in the elementary grades was especially awed by his ability to arrive at the right answers through his own unorthodox method, which never followed his teacher's procedure. His English teacher in Grade 5, who was always devising ways to catch him unprepared, as he always seemed distracted, never quite succeeded; he knew the correct answers even if he seemed not to be paying attention. He often got into trouble in class because of his disruptive behavior, but his teachers generally admitted that despite his troubles, he was among the best in class performance.

Even as a young boy, Popot developed a reputation for being a tough guy. He was one of the smallest in his class, but that did not deter him from beating up the bigger boys if they crossed him. Even the upperclassmen steered clear of him. He was especially protective of his older brother who was a year ahead in class and was sometimes a target for bullies. One time, he beat up a bully in his older brother's class, a boy much bigger than he was. That was his way of telling all the other bullies to keep off his brother. Nobody messes up with a crazy guy, and for most of his peers, he was a crazy guy.

His behavior underwent a dramatic change when we transferred to California. He was in Grade 8 when we migrated to the United States. The gregarious, ever-moving dynamo of a boy with reckless disregard for personal safety disappeared. Popot became the reclusive loner whose two destinations were school and home. He did not go out with friends as his older brother did. He hated going out, especially to the shopping malls. His main interests outside of class were limited to television, movies, the Internet, and trading cards. He was still doing exceptionally well in his classes, but at home he spent very little time preparing for his classes, unlike his older brother who would study late into the night. At nine in the evening, Popot would be hitting the sack.

Even in school, teachers noticed the considerable differences between Voltaire and his brother Hamlet. While Hamlet oozed with ambition and supported this with hard work, Voltaire would be a far cry with his laid-back attitude and the ease with which he attacked his academic chores. Hamlet was the gregarious student who liked to hang around with his friends in and out of class while Voltaire was the brooding loner who liked to stay in a corner all by his lonesome or in the silent company of other brooding loners. Some of the more perceptive teachers saw through the brothers' differences to the essential intellectual gifts of the siblings. There were some teachers who in fact regarded Voltaire as the more naturally talented of the two brothers, his weird ways notwithstanding.

CHAPTER 12

SLEEPER

She was the unexpected child, born when her mother was already forty. We had always wanted a daughter, even after our first son. We had mistakenly read the signs of the second pregnancy as indicating that we would have a daughter, and we were mildly disappointed when we found out that our second child was a boy. We tried to have another child, hoping that it would be a girl, but for quite a long time we were unsuccessful.

When my wife was in her late thirties, we had given up hope about having another child, especially because of the danger associated with such pregnancy. Her obstetrician had warned her earlier that many possible complications arise from a pregnancy at a later age. We had a friend who became pregnant in her forties, whose child was born with Downe syndrome.

When my wife was nearing forty, she experienced constant headaches, prompting her to see a doctor. She came back from the doctor strangely happy about what she discovered. She broke the good news that we were going to have a daughter. I myself was not quite comfortable with the news because of the possible attendant difficulties that it may bring. True enough, at five months she experienced pain in the stomach area, which upon examination showed that she was already partially dilated, with the possibility that the baby would be born prematurely. She was advised by the obstetrician to stop working and rest in bed until the birth of the baby.

When she was six months pregnant, I had a heart attack while playing basketball with friends and had to stay in the ICU of a hospital for two weeks plus another two weeks in a regular hospital room, for recovery. That was a traumatic experience for my wife, as we had no relatives in Indonesia who could help her cope with the problems she had to face simultaneously.

Lara was born under difficult circumstances. Physically I was a shadow of my former athletic self. I was constantly in poor health and very irritable, especially with my two sons who had not yet quite understood what had happened to change me so drastically. I was worried about everything: my health, my work, our finances, and my future with the company I was working for. But Lara was also the source of happiness for everybody in the family when everything else seemed bleak. Her features were almost identical with my own in the pictures we had of me as a baby, having a round face with big innocent eyes. It was as if there was a certain symbolism in what was happening: new life replacing old life. She was a bubbly little baby who smiled most of the time as if she was born a happy girl with a positive outlook in life.

Even as a small tot, she was sweet and talkative, prompting the maid who had cared for my two sons since they were babies to state that she was probably the most intelligent of the three.

Actually, her initial performance in education was not very encouraging. At three, we sent her to a playgroup called *Lollipop School* where the teachers and owner prided themselves in having "advanced" students. After several months, my wife and I noticed that Lara hated school, making all kinds of excuses to miss it. My wife and I investigated what seemed to be the problem. To her horror, my wife discovered that the teachers were imposing on the children a very past pace, with so much advanced material to cover that even six-year-olds would have difficulty digesting them. No wonder our daughter had beady sweats in the evenings when we talked to her about school. During class recitation, Lara was almost in tears, as she could not quite follow the pace of the other children in answering math questions in oral competition, which was the style the math teacher preferred.

My wife and I discussed Lara's predicament and possible ways out. We knew she had completely lost confidence in her abilities because of the school's system, and we had paid the school good money to do that to her. The next task was to look for a school that would restore her self-confidence through re-affirmation.

We found a school run by an American lady named Susan where the philosophy of educating was completely child-oriented. It was called the *Little Apple School*. We talked to Susan about Lara's special need and what we were looking for. Susan assured us her school was the right fit for Lara. Slowly, Lara recovered her self-confidence. It came to a point where she would volunteer to stand up in front of everybody to show what she had learned. By the time she had finished school there, she seemed to have forgotten her bad experience with her previous school. She again showed composure, and we were thankful to the new school for their patience in mending her shattered confidence.

Lara left *Little Apple* in the wake of the economic crisis in Indonesia. The local currency, the *Rupiah*, had devalued to a fifth of its previous value, prompting the employers of expatriate managers to stop paying the equivalent of their dollar wages. Since schooling of the children was paid in dollars, a good number of expatriates were forced to go home to their countries when the incomes became lower than the basic expenses. In our case, we had to take the kids out of international schools and enroll them in local schools. We expected to be migrating to America in a year or two so, in the case of Lara, we did not want to send her to a local school where they taught using Indonesian as the medium of instruction. Instead, we decided to enroll her in a Japanese-style course named *Kumon* that taught both mathematics and English in an intensive way. By the end of 12 months, Lara was proficient in both Math and English, which was our short-term objective anyway. She had enough time to devote to gymnastics where we also enrolled her, as the gym was only about 10 minutes away from the house. She could do the daily workouts at the gym, lasting two hours and a half as required of the trainees, and still attend her classes.

A year later, my wife found a local school for rich Indonesians where the medium of instruction was English. An Australian lady ran this school, and the teachers were English-speaking Indonesians. Tuition was quite high by Indonesian standards but significantly lower than in the international schools. Again, this proved to be a confidence-booster for Lara as she found that among her classmates in grade one, she was the most advanced in both Math and English. Lara stayed in that school for only 6 months as we received our immigration documents and had to leave for California within three months.

As soon as we arrived in Hayward, California, we enrolled Lara in a private Catholic school. Although it was the middle of the school year, she was accepted without any problems. This proved to be another confidence-booster again for Lara, as at the end of the school year, she was the top student in her class. But the 300 dollars a month was too much for our family to keep up with as only my wife was working at the time, prompting us to decide to transfer her to a public school the next year.

Lara enjoyed her transfer to a public school located very near the house we temporarily lived in. Gone were the uniforms of the private school. It also helped that she had for a second grade teacher a bubbly woman who was the favorite of students, even by former students. Lara adored her. The two still keep in touch with each other, never forgetting each other's birthday. If there is such a thing as a second mother, Ms. DeJulio would be a second mother to Lara and to many of her students.

In third grade, Lara had a very efficient teacher who accomplished everything that she promised she would do that year. She planned all her activities for the year and efficiently executed them according to her plan. Although not as warm and as well–liked by her students as Lara's second grade teacher, she was nevertheless very good for Lara's intellectual development because of her almost managerial efficiency in handling her third grade class.

Lara's fourth and fifth grade teachers did not do as well for Lara as her previous two. The subject matters that she and her classmates took up in the next two years were often rehashed from the previous years. Lara was fortunate to have continued with a special course in math outside formal school through which she has been able to maintain three-years-over-grade-level proficiency. This ensured that her math skills continued to develop, albeit off-campus.

When we transferred to California, we were eager to have Lara continue with her gymnastics training as she had made quite some progress there while we were still in Jakarta. Initially, we enrolled her in a gymnastics course for Tuesday and Thursday sessions. I was still unemployed when she re-started gymnastics so I was the designated driver for her trips to the gym. Bringing her there from our house became a major concern as soon as I started working. No one was available to replace me so eventually we had to settle for a Saturday session at another facility so either her mother or I could bring her without conflict of schedule. From then on, the infrequent sessions coupled with her own physical growth combined to cause a plateau of sort in her gymnastics skills development.

Another course that Lara started in Jakarta was swimming. She used to tag along with her mother to a fitness center in downtown Jakarta that had a good-sized swimming pool with a swimming instructor. While still in Jakarta, she learned freestyle, a little bit of breaststroke, and treading water. When we moved to Hayward, California, her eldest brother Hamlet joined a competitive swimming club and participated in the Hayward Swim Fest during the summer of 2000. He won several medals and received a trophy from his coach for the most improved swimmer of his swimming club. Motivated by his early achievements, he went on for further training and became a lifeguard at the local swimming center. Because her brother was a part-time lifeguard at the center, Lara was exempted from regular enrollment fees for swimming courses. She re-started her swimming course in 2001 and from then on, became a regular swimming student at the facility, progressing from level 1 in 2001 to level 6 in 2004.

During the school year 2003-2004, Lara distinguished herself in several fronts. She was consistently the top student in her grade 5 class, became the Spelling Bee champion of the school, received a GOLD STAR award from her special off-campus math course called KUMON for being 3 years ahead of her grade level, and during the summer of 2004, she won two gold medals, one silver medal, and one bronze medal from the citywide age-group swimming competition.

It was during that summer of 2004 when, after observing Lara during their four-week training sessions, her swimming coach Glenn

Morimoto told my wife Del that Lara, like her brother Hamlet a few years back, "is a sleeper".

Asked what he meant, Glenn explained that Lara has it in her to win competitions although she does not know it herself yet. He explained further that there are things that mark a winner that coaches cannot teach; it is in the nature of that person, and only an experienced eye can see it.

Among our children, Lara may yet prove to be the real sleeper. I suppose the winner in her had always been there; it just took her mom and me a bit longer to finally see it in her.

When she was struggling at the age of three, my wife and I entertained the thought that indeed we might have a dumb child, but *we did not give up.* We did everything in our power to help her get over her seemingly insurmountable problems because *as parents we could not accept the possibility of failing her.* Her incredible comebacks vindicated our faith in her ability to overcome obstacles.

I am happy to tell the reader that Lara has finally found her stride, and she may yet surpass the achievements of her older brothers.

PART 5:
INFLUENTIAL PERSONAGES

CHAPTER 13

CHERISHED MENTOR

Among the many influential mentors that nurtured me, one stood out. As I was writing the other chapters of this book, I made a mental note to devote a special chapter to him. I wanted the piece to sound very personal; hence, my decision to use the open letter format. I titled it "A Letter to A Cherished Mentor".

"Father Vincent, you will probably not remember me even if I told you my name. I was your student in third year high school at the Christ the King Seminary in Quezon City, in the Philippines, way back in 1963.

I now live here in the United States, more specifically in Hayward, California, with my wife and three children. My eldest, a son, is a senior at Stanford University while my second eldest, another son, is a junior at the University of Southern California in Los Angeles. My youngest, a daughter at last, is in eighth grade preparing for her entry into high school. We came here as immigrants some seven years ago to join my mother and my other siblings, who had preceded us here in the 1980s.

I came by way of Jakarta, Indonesia, where I lived and worked some eighteen years before coming to the United States.

I was a classmate of Tony Pernia, who, I gathered, has become the top man of the SVD. I left (was made to leave, technically) the SVD seminary in Tagaytay (a remote scenic city in Cavite) in 1971, after I finished the one-year academic course for my masters in Philosophy. Fr. Willie Villegas, a classmate of the more famous Ed de la Torre and Bishop Vic Manuel, is my first-degree cousin.

I "googled" you a few weeks ago and was pleasantly surprised to know that you are still alive somewhere in San Antonio, Texas, in a home for retired priests, and still actively ministering to a community. I became quite curious and tried to look for your picture through the Internet. I did see a picture of you and some of the other retired priests posted in the Internet but the picture was so small I couldn't make out how you actually look now.

I remember you were a handsome young priest, albeit balding, in 1963. I can't forget your round bright eyes and your earnest smiling face. I actually purchased a. second-hand copy of your book, *The Lord and I*, through Amazon, and there it was, your familiar face, some ten years older than the one I remember, facing me from its back cover

My wife, a sociology graduate from the University of Santo Tomas in Manila, had read some parts of your book as it came through the mail before I even knew it had arrived. She thinks you are a bit conservative in your ideas, but she liked your clear, simple style of writing. She is fifty-five years old now, three years younger than I am. Diagnosed with 4th stage breast cancer some 19 months ago, she has been on long term disability since then. She still tries to keep herself active by constantly renovating and redecorating our mobile home and tending to her plants, but her strength only lasts half a day.

My three unmarried sisters, two older and one younger, have been very kind to us, bringing dinner to our house every night to help out in our time of temporary inconvenience. I always consider it a temporary inconvenience because one way or the other it will be resolved permanently. Anyway, one of my sisters was curious about your book when she saw it on our dinner table and borrowed it after I had scan-read only some parts of it. She liked it so much she asked me to purchase two more copies to give to some priest-friends here. Oh yes, you have some incidental fans here now.

You don't know it but you were one of the major influences in my development as a person. I always wanted to tell you that you were my ideal teacher, the one who stands out among the best I had.

I remember the teacher who made us read seven books in one year: Jack London's *The Call of the Wild*, Charles Dickens' *A Tale of Two Cities,* and another author's *Ben Hur,* to name three that I still remember. I remember quite vividly the characters in Shakespeare's *Merchant of Venice*: Shylock and his consuming desire for vengeance, for a pound of Antonio's flesh; the proud Antonio and his devotion to his male friend; the witty Portia who brought Shylock back to earth with her guile. I can hear you in my memory reading that Shakespearean play. *You made them real to me in the classroom.*

But what I really want to thank you for were the poems. When you read them to us, they sprang to life. Those poems have been my inspirations in life. I can still picture in my memory God as the hound of heaven relentlessly pursuing the writer in Francis Bacon's hauntingly glorious poem *The Hound of Heaven.* I can picture Edwin Markham's man with the hoe, he with the empty look and slanted brows, and I can understand the poet's protestations to the rulers of the world. I still remember how I felt as you recited Carl Sandburg's poems about the grass (with its allusions to Austerlitz and Waterloo) and Chicago (butcher of the world), and I consider those to be your best performances ever. Thanks to you I memorized Shakespeare's Sonnet XXIX and can still recite it by heart. I can imagine the blind Milton, no longer despondent but proud, standing still and waiting, doing his daylight labor. I can vividly see Robert Frost taking the less trodden road (as I often did) or walking miles and miles on a snowy evening. *Those are unforgettable vignettes from the mind of an impressionable young student of yours.*

I also remember the respect you gave us in handling our quizzes. Every time you gave a quiz, you corrected them immediately and gave them back to us the next day. *No overwork excuse.* You even added a small gift to the student who did the best. I remember because I got some of those token gifts. You may not have realized it, but those small recognitions went a long way. I still talk about my ideal teacher to my friends and family.

After I left the seminary, I taught Philosophy for a year at the College of the Holy Spirit in Manila. After that, I taught one semester at St. Theresa's College in Quezon City. President Marcos' declaration of martial law in 1972 cut short my budding teaching career. But the itch to teach continued. (My mother was my grade six teacher, but it was you who inspired me most to teach.) After I obtained my MBA degree at the De La Salle University in 1979, I taught for a year again at the Philippine Women's University. In 1980, a year before I left for Jakarta, Indonesia, I taught for a year at the College of St. Scholastica, at the invitation of Mario Bolasco, a classmate and dear friend from Tagaytay who was Chairman of the Philosophy Department of the college (and who passed away in 1992). I again taught for a year at an MBA school in Jakarta. I have not taught for some time now, but I have promised myself that after I retire, I will go back to the Philippines and teach English to high school students the way I remember you teaching it.

I was studying philosophy in the late 60s and the early 70s, taught by teachers who probably thought quite differently from you or your teachers. That is why you would seem to me far more conservative than I am, and I would seem to you far more liberal than your thinking. (I offer no value judgments here.) In Tagaytay, our class came under the academic influence of John Fullenbach, a German SVD priest who was also teaching Fundamental Theology and who later taught at the Gregorian University in Rome. Under him, we developed interest in Kant and Hegel and a whole slew of German philosophers like Feuerbach, Marx, Nietzsche, and Heidegger. I myself developed a special liking for Nietzsche and Camus, two very troubling but quite fascinating writers.

At the same time, Mario Bolasco, Tony Pernia, and myself had become more and more involved in organizational work with the farmers of Cavite and Central Luzon. (Developments in the Philippines were bound to impact even our sheltered lives inevitably.) That involvement in social justice work made me more vocal and contentious in my interactions with seminary authorities and my peers that ultimately led to my expulsion from Tagaytay.

I have often revisited that issue in my own musings. From my perspective now, I would not have done it any other way. Through my involvement in social justice work, I realized that if I were going to become a priest, I would be a priest for the poor. Before that, I seemed to have lost my bearings. I was experiencing a jarring disconnect between what I felt I was becoming and what Jesus would have been doing. I no longer had the taste for the rituals of the priesthood and was looking for more in terms of commitment and focus. I had always competed for academic honors enthusiastically but I was finding that it was for no other glorious purpose but my personal glory. Like many of my classmates and friends inside, I was troubled and listless. I was in crisis, and Camus and Nietzsche seemed very appealing. My involvement with the farmers gave me back my focus. It, however, alienated me from the people around me. To my peers and my superiors, I must have looked like a mad dog, ranting about a struggle that they could not understand and could not care about. That did not sit well with them. Eventually, I was voted out.

I can now look back and be philosophical about it. I am happy now. I cannot see myself happier despite the difficulties that I have come to accept as part of life. Would I have been happier as a priest? It is a moot question now, but I feel deep down that I would probably have been miserable.

I do not say this to disparage people like you whom I admire. I left the seminary, but I did not leave the church. I like to think of myself as belonging to the left wing of the church, not very obedient, critical of many of its practices, but a true believer. In the end, when I do face the great hound of heaven, I believe I can explain myself."

CHAPTER 14

THE MAN I ADMIRED MOST

He was a most ordinary man. If I had not known him personally, he would have been just one of the two hundred twenty million Indonesians that didn't matter to me. I was a Filipino expatriate in Jakarta, and my exposure to ordinary Indonesians was very limited.

Tatang was our family driver for some three years, our fifth driver in the first seven years of our stay in Indonesia. At the time he was our driver, we owned a fifteen-year-old Toyota Corona that Tatang drove to bring my eldest son Hamlet to playschool some thirty minutes away from the house. I drove to the office a three-year-old Daihatsu Charade that my office leased for my use. After bringing back my son to our house at noontime, Tatang used public transport to our office where he waited to drive me back to our house at night. My wife was also working, and for that, her office sent a car to fetch her in the morning and bring her back to the house in the afternoon. My wife and I could concentrate fully on our work because we had three maids to take care

95

of the household chores that included caring for our two very young sons and preparing meals for the family.

Tatang was a very dependable driver and companion to our eldest son so much so that we trusted our three-year-old son to his care as we pursued our very busy daily schedules. My wife reached home at six in the evening while I would be back at home usually at nine in the evening, and once a week, at twelve in the evening. With his always-happy disposition, Tatang was a perfect uncle to my sons, and we treated him as family.

When my contract with SC Johnson expired in 1988, my wife and two sons went back to Manila. We had planned to stay there for good. I followed them a month later, but I had to go back to Jakarta in two weeks for consultancy with Brataco, a local company. I had agreed to a six-month consultancy with the local company with no assurance that there was anything more permanent. I retained one of the maids and Tatang during that period of uncertainty. What initially was an awkward six-month consultancy turned out to be a longer-term hiring for me when Brataco's owner asked me to bring my family back to Jakarta. They had been in Manila only nine months.

This interim setup unnerved Tatang so much that he began looking for another job even as I started my consultancy. I was into my third month in my six-month consultancy with Brataco when he disappeared without giving notice. A few days later, he sent his wife to the executive suite of my friend, where I was temporarily residing, with a letter explaining his decision to find a more stable place of work. I understood very well his feeling of uncertainty and told his wife that everything was okay. I still considered him a friend. I knew he was feeling guilty, but his getting another job was no big thing for me.

When my wife and children joined me again in Jakarta, Tatang continued to drop by our house to say hello. On one of those occasions, he looked pale and weak. He explained that he was undergoing weekly blood transfusion as he had been diagnosed with a blood disorder known as Aplastic Anemia. On another occasion, he related how his wife had encouraged him to go back to his father's house, as she couldn't take care of him anymore.

It was not long before we heard that his wife had left him for another man, bringing with her their two children. Yet, through all these personal misfortunes, Tatang did not show any rancor or anger for what he had to undergo. He remained calm, seemingly untouched by the world that seemed to be caving in on him.

Even with his weekly sessions at the blood transfusion clinic, Tatang continued to report to work. Once he came by our house to borrow seed money for a buy-and-sell small business he wanted to start in his workplace. I had known him for his honesty so it was no problem for us. At that time, he was one of our close friends, and not being employed by us made it less awkward for us to be friends. He had kept in close touch with my children who looked up to him as their distant "uncle".

One early morning, we received a call from a woman who told us she was Tatang's sister. She had sad news for us. Tatang passed away in the middle of the night. As was the custom for Muslims, he would be buried early afternoon that day. His body was at his father's house.

I took that day off from work and brought our whole household, my wife and three kids, our two drivers and their respective cars, even our three maids who had known Tatang, to the West Java town where Tatang's body was being prepared for burial. There, I met his father, whom I had never met before. He had tears in his eyes, but his first concern was the money that his son owed me. I told him to forget about the money. Tatang was my friend, and I was there to grieve with them. I wept as I clasped his hands. It was the first time I had ever wept for a dead person. I did not do it for my father when he died. I did not do it for my best friend when he died.

Tatang was a most beautiful gift to me. He taught me a lot of things about life, the simple unadulterated life that decent men live. I had always been proud of how I had lived my life, but beside him, I felt dwarfed.

He was not angry with God for the misfortunes he had to deal with. He did not hate his wife who left him for another man. In fact, he was willing to take her back with no questions. He had an inner strength that was unequaled by any man I had known. When people talk of saints, I just smile. I had known one, and he was not even a Christian.

CHAPTER 15

GEORGE GODINEZ

efore I ever met him, I was terrified of George. He was the type of person whose reputation was intimidating. George was my tenant when I was property manager of Caltrans-owned houses in Hayward, California.

I had been in the United States for only a year, and I was anxious to get a job. The first institution willing to take a chance in hiring me was California's Department of Transportation (Caltrans). I had applied to so many companies, but nothing seemed to pan out so when I was offered to join the Department as a right of way agent, I snapped up the opportunity.

My first assignment was in property management. I had no previous specific training for the job, but I was determined to be good at it by using a lot of common sense and the skills I had acquired from working as a business manager in the Philippines and Indonesia. And property management turned out to be tailor-made for me, a very enjoyable and satisfying type of work for someone starting a second career.

As I reviewed the thick file that was George's tenancy records, I was struck by the seeming aggressiveness of the guy. Page after page chronicled a history of animosity with previous property managers, including the lady I replaced. I made a mental note to place him at the bottom of the list of tenants to meet for the annual inspection. I did not want to deal with the difficult type before I had enough experience with the less difficult ones.

When I finally had to talk to him over the phone to schedule the inspection of his residence, I did so with much apprehension. To my surprise, he was not as gruff as I imagined he would be. In fact, he sounded soft-spoken. When I did make my visit to his house, I was expecting a big man to meet me at his door and was mildly surprised to find a man about my size, much thinner than myself, smiling as he opened the door.

George had been a tenant of Caltrans for some thirty years, one of the longest staying in the Hayward area. The tenancy was supposed to be short and temporary, as the land had been purchased from the owners for a highway project. Demolition and construction was to follow in a few months after acquisition by Caltrans, but the project was put on hold and never resurrected. By the time I joined the property management group, some tenants in the Hayward area had been renting for some thirty years. George's residence was built in the early 1900s in a relatively large piece of land uncharacteristic of the other real properties in the neighborhood. As I entered the house, I noticed the outdated shaggy-type carpet that reflected the age of the house. I was a bit surprised to see that the carpet looked clean in a way that indicated that it had always been kept clean. It had not deteriorated in the same way other newer carpets had in the other houses I had visited.

I walked through the entire house with George, noting down the things that needed repair. The facilities were old, like the bathtub that was located in the open space near the kitchen. I also noticed the almost clinical neatness of the whole place, and I felt a certain respect for its resident.

Contrary to my expectation, George was polite. Even as he made requests for items like the new shower and shower curtain and repair of the wooden deck at the back, he was courteous. We got to talk about our high school sons and their sports activities in-between the official tenant-landlord talk, striking a certain warmth between two proud fathers. As I walked away from his house later, I felt foolish for having prejudged the man so wrongly.

I had promised George several improvements in his house, which I quickly delivered in the following weeks after the inspection. Every time something I promised was done, he would call to thank me, leaving a message in my voice mail if I was not there. Somehow we developed mutual respect. I delivered on my promises, and he called to acknowledge and thank me.

A few months after the inspection, George was laid off from work. I did not know it at first. He called me up on the tenth of the month, which is the deadline for rent payment, to inform me that he would be late with the payment for that month but that he would pay the rent for two months on the first week of the next month. He told me he was selling one of the vintage cars in his collection to raise the money. The next month, he delivered on his promise. I called him to thank him. This would happen three times in the period that I was property manager of his residence. He always delivered as he promised.

When I was told that I was being transferred to the Appraisals section, I sent a letter to all my tenants telling them of my impending transfer and introducing my replacement. George was one of those who called me to thank me for my work. He said that he was sad that I was leaving my property management work, saying that I was the first one from Caltrans to have treated him with respect. I almost winced at hearing it because I thought what I did was nothing spectacular. That was the last time I heard from George.

One fateful afternoon when I was at the thirteenth floor lobby waiting for the elevator to bring me down on my way home, I chanced to meet my former superior in property management. Almost casually he mentioned to me that the previous night a fire had gutted George's residence while he was asleep inside. Unfortunately, George had perished with the house.

From what I gathered later, people who knew him better said that George had a lot of self-created problems. It was even mentioned that he was drunk the night his house caught fire. People who never met him in person but read his thick tenancy file would conclude that he was a nasty person in much the same way I imagined before I met him. In the few moments that I shared with him, I had a glimpse of a decent man. That was the George Godinez I knew.

Chapter 16

My Special Gift

I experienced a strange sort of awakening a few days after undergoing a double-bypass surgery in Perth, Australia, when complications were happening one after another. For a while, I thought I was going to succumb to one of those and join my friend Mario on the other side. It was then that I mentally promised myself that if I lived through that ordeal, I will re-organize my priorities in life the way I was seeing it from what seemed to be my deathbed. I always look back to that fateful time as my epiphany.

From then on, I started looking at the proximate world around me with new eyes, noticing a lot more things, being kinder to the people around me, regarding problems as opportunities for self-growth, valuing the bonus time that I was enjoying. People in need were no longer problems to be avoided but gifts provided for self-sanctification. Suddenly the world was brighter and infinitely more challenging because dealing with it and its myriad problems had become quite meaningful.

This was forcefully brought to me by the case of Russell. He was a tenant in one of the houses I was managing for the State in Hayward, California. Russell, a retired barber in his late seventies, was a Native American, a Pomo Indian specifically. Living on a monthly pension of six hundred dollars, he was paying 196 dollars a month for the two-room house he was living in under the hard-case program of the State. He had rented the house for some thirty years by the time I started managing it.

I met Russell the first time when I conducted the annual inspection of his house. That was a few weeks after his neighbor Violeta, also my tenant, passed away. Violeta was the original owner of both the house where she died in and the house Russell occupied. Violeta's husband was Russell's longtime customer and friend who was instrumental in renting the house to Russell. When Violeta's husband died, Russell took it on himself to regularly look after the aging Violeta.

I instinctively liked Russell when I met him. He was my idea of the grandfather that I never met. He had plenty of stories to tell about his younger days, and even at his advanced age, he was light-spirited and did not show any tinge of bitterness I usually associate with old people. Despite the creases on his face, he seemed generally happy with himself.

One day, I received a call from a social worker informing me that Russell was at the Eden Medical Center in Castro Valley, the hospital nearest his house. The story was that Russell's next-door neighbor, seeing Russell's newspapers lying around untended on his front yard, had barged in through the front door, finding Russell unconscious in his bathroom. He was lying on his face and had been in that position for some days. I learned through the social worker that Russell's closest kin was a daughter in Florida who was also ailing.

I visited Russell at the hospital where I learned more about what happened. He told me that during his last visit to his doctor, the doctor advised him to go on a diet as he was putting on more weight. Thinking that the best way to diet was to limit his food intake to liquids, he sustained himself for several days on just drinking bottled Sprite. He progressively became weaker and weaker until his legs could no longer support his upper body. He collapsed one morning in the bathroom and was there for three days until his neighbor Michael, also my tenant, barged in and found him.

Russell told me that aside from me, he had only two other visitors. His ex-wife, who now lives in another state, learned from their daughter about his situation and rushed to his bedside. It had been a long while since their divorce and the last time he had seen her. I could see the gleam in his eyes as he talked about her. She was now married to another man with whom she had other children. A hint of regret crossed his face as he related how he lost her through uncontrolled drinking. He smiled a bit as he remembered the reckless days of his youth that proved to be his undoing.

The other hospital visitor was Manuel, his businessman boss and friend from his barbering days before retirement. Manuel would occasionally visit him at his house, and on one of those days, he learned from Michael the neighbor that Russell was at the hospital. Manuel was the guy who would straighten things out for Russell, sometimes financially, when Russell would experience some dire need. It was Manuel who fixed the arrangements at the hospital. I met Manuel several days after my hospital visit when by chance we both went to Russell's house to fix some things.

When the social worker first informed me about Russell's hospitalization, she also told me that Russell was afraid he would lose the house he was renting from the State. I told her to pass on the message that he should not worry about it and should concentrate on getting well. I will make sure he does not lose the house. I was thinking that since he was paying only a monthly rent of 196 dollars, he could easily pay for it from his 600 dollars monthly pension. After talking to Manuel, I learned that Russell's entire pension was being paid to the hospital, along with the additional contributions from Medicaid, for the duration of his hospitalization. I also knew that the State would evict Russell if he failed to pay his monthly rent.

I thought of talking to my supervisor to explain the situation, but I was sure it would have been to no avail. It bothered me that we would have to evict an old man because he was hospitalized. I thought back to the time when I was in Perth, Australia, begging the heart surgeon, whose schedule was fully booked for four weeks, to put me in his schedule or I would die. I must have looked desperate then, feeling that the whole world had caved in on me. It was only then that I understood the meaning of compassion when the surgeon, who did not know me from Adam, decided on the spot to give up his Saturday with his family and operate on me two days from that fateful meeting in his office. *I was his special gift, the perfect opportunity to help, to do good in a special way.* When he faces the last judge, I just know my case will stand out because he showed compassion.

Russell was my special gift. I was placed in a unique position where I was the only one who could have done anything. I had two thousand dollars in the bank that I had saved to buy a laptop computer. If I used it to pay for the rent, Russell could stay in the hospital for ten months without losing his house. Russell stayed in the hospital for eight months. The rent got paid for eight months. Russell did not even know how I fixed it.

The Greeks have a word about the opportune time. It is *kairos*. Meeting Russell was my kairos.

If I look back and regard my near-death experience in Perth, Australia, as my epiphany, my experience with Russell was comparable to Paul's incident on the road to Damascus. It showed me a parallel world, the world of gifts.

CHAPTER 17

CANDLES IN THE DARK

I was still living in Jakarta, Indonesia, when I witnessed on television the fall from power of the country's strongman, General Suharto, in 1998, as the students demonstrated in the streets to force his ouster. It was a momentous event, something nobody could have predicted six months earlier, when he had absolute control of the country's political and military power structures.

This exercise of people power to topple a tyrant was actually a repeat of what happened earlier in Manila in 1986, when the Philippines' civilian dictator Ferdinand Marcos fell from power.

I lived under both regimes and personally witnessed the excesses of both leaders.

I was a young philosophy teacher in a Catholic college in 1972 when Marcos declared martial law, consolidating his hold on all the power structures of the country. I lost my job as a consequence of his directive to heads of schools to terminate all faculty members that they could not personally vouch for. To ensure the loyalty of the Philippine military, Marcos lavishly provided the top officers with financial favors. He rewarded his friends and relatives with lucrative deals. Government banks were raided to fund white-elephant business projects that were designed to funnel money outside the country into private bank accounts of Marcos associates. In short, Marcos basically streamlined corruption. It was with a sigh of relief that I accepted employment abroad in 1981, thankful for the opportunity to be rid of the repressive conditions in the Philippines.

I arrived in Jakarta, Indonesia, at the time when the country was swimming in a sea of petrodollars that was a windfall from the high price of oil, the country's main export commodity. This was the time when Indonesia was on the verge of an economic takeoff.

General Suharto had taken over the reins of government in the late 1960s from the country's charismatic founding father Sukarno, who had been implicated in the failed coup attempt of 1965. The country's government bureaucracy was completely militarized, with the majority of the provinces run by governors who were retired generals and with the cabinet ministers, with the exception of a few, also retired generals. One could see everywhere the unmistakable signs of idol-worship, with billboards prominently showing the smiling general, whose ruthless rule belied his genial face. People talked in whisper to me as they repeated stories about acts of repression that they heard about or witnessed themselves. The adoring slogans and public praises notwithstanding, one could sense the fear of and silent repugnance for the tyrant by the people, even though revealed only in hushed voices asking for anonymity.

Flare-ups occasionally happened as it did in early 1982 in the run up to the general election when rioting and looting showed their ugly heads in Jakarta, the country's prime city. The most memorable of these early manifestations of dissent was in 1983 when the military garrison in Tanjung Priok was attacked by unarmed rioters, which incident was followed by the hush-hush massacre of the unarmed attackers. The official report set the casualty number at fifty, but the unofficial consensus was that the actual number was many times over the officially acknowledged number.

The influential mass media always deferred to the government version of events. The iron hand of the government came down mercilessly whenever dissent or criticism of the ruling clique was apparent. Kompas and Suara Pembaharuan, the two leading daily newspapers, were cowed into printing only praises for the ruling elite. No critical phrase or sentence was tolerated on print.

Suharto's family gradually took prominence, starting with his wife, Madame Tien. She started to exert influence in all phases of Indonesian life. She became the patroness of the arts. All major social occasions had to be graced by her. Health programs had to have her *imprimatur*. She even pressured the government to do away with the polygamous practice among government officials.

Suharto's children followed, monopolizing business ventures. The country's freeway system was privatized in favor of his eldest daughter Tutut. Yearly increases in toll fees were mandated solely to fill up the coffers of the company she owned. The booming clove industry was privatized to favor Suharto's youngest son Tommy. Commercial television stations were allowed to operate, but Suharto's children had to be the majority stockholders. Competing supermarket chains had to have equity from his children. Every business, to be substantially big, had to have his children's equity and protection. It came to a point when the country appeared to be Suharto's private business. Everybody who was not in his economic loop was secretly seething with indignation but suffered in stoic silence.

It was into this scene that two men were pushed into prominence in 1996.

The first of these was Muchtar Pakpahan, a labor leader. Against the directive of the government that only government-sanctioned unions could organize, he organized a labor union of mainly bus drivers that the government refused to sanction. He was subjected to so much intimidation, yet instead of backing down, he dared to speak out in public against the government in general and the president in particular. For that, he was thrown in prison for sedition.

The other person was Sri Bintang Pamungkas, a professor of Economics at the University of Indonesia. He was elected as a legislator under the United Development Party, one of the three parties recognized by the government. Instead of towing the party line of quietly endorsing the government's initiatives, he spoke out in public forums against the excesses of the president and his cohorts. He was the only politician who dared to criticize the government in public. For that, he was thrown in prison for sedition. He lost his professorship at the public university; his family members became outcasts in their community and reduced to depending on their kin for their financial needs.

It was at about this time when the news of their public opposition to the president and their subsequent imprisonment was the talk of the people that my driver Rasam asked me, somewhat rhetorically, why these two people would be so stupid as to do what they did. I remember telling him, somewhat emotionally because the issue touched the core of my own existence, that these two men were candles in the dark, that through their lonely lights other people would light their own candles, knowing that they were not alone anymore in their indignation. It was a little too personal for me because I was starting to believe that I was alone in my indignation at the things that were transpiring in that country. I had found two people among two hundred million willing to go to prison for their convictions. It was both comforting and reassuring.

Two years after Muchtar and Bintang went to prison, in 1998, what was deemed impossible actually happened. Suharto came crashing down. Muchtar and Bintang were released from their prison in Cipinang, East Jakarta, their faith vindicated, their sacrifices finally appreciated. On that day, I had a chance to talk to my driver Rasam again. I reminded him about my comment two years earlier about these men being candles in the dark. Those two lonely lights started a conflagration that even the mighty Suharto, with all his minions, could not really put out. I do not know if Rasam saw it the way I saw it.

I was not in Manila in 1986 when Marcos fell, but two of my sisters were at EDSA (Epifanio de los Santos Avenue) when he finally went to exile in Hawaii. I was in Jakarta at the time, reading the telexes about the rebellion at the Sari Pacific Hotel. I did not actually see the events unfold, but I was there in spirit, even as those who criticized and laughed at us when we opposed Marcos some two decades earlier were in EDSA participating in toppling Marcos. I could relate to Muchtar and Bintang because I was one of the few in the late sixties and the early seventies holding lonely candles in opposition to Marcos.

I need to point out here that Muchtar was Christian while Bintang was Muslim, but it was not their religious affiliations that stood out at their hour of heroism; rather, it was their shared commitment to truth and decency, stifling their fears of brutal retribution, that marked them at their finest hour. It underscored the most important point that regardless of our differences, we all share a common humanity that has no borders.

PART 6:
TRANSITION 2

CHAPTER 18

RELOCATION INCONVENIENCES

When my family and I arrived in Hayward, California, as immigrants at the end of 1999, we were forced to crash in the house of my mother and sisters. We were not really penniless, but practically homeless.

My wife and I had gambled on coming to America, away from a comfortable life in Jakarta, Indonesia, where I had established myself as a successful business executive, primarily because we wanted our three children to have access to America's renowned schools of learning. We had battled our self-doubts, telling ourselves that we were doing the right thing because we believed in *the dream*, the American dream that *everything is possible*.

We had brought all our eighteen years' savings of eighty thousand dollars from Jakarta to ensure we would not starve as we started a new life here. Both my wife and I were unemployed at the start, with very little idea of where our work skills would fit.

I was a *classic* marketing executive in the Unilever (the multinational consumer products company) brand management mold in Manila and Jakarta, but the Bay Area where we settled in was all about *high-tech* marketing, so I felt like fish out of water. Each job interview I went to was progressively humiliating, until my self-confidence had almost ebbed away completely. I had all these successful experiences in Manila and Jakarta as a business manager, but nobody seemed to believe I was telling the truth, that I was capable of doing the things that I said I did. It was basically the same with my wife; she was a university-based sociologist in Manila and Jakarta for 18 years. To transition herself from the academe to the business world, she had worked as market research analyst in a securities company in our last two years in Jakarta.

In our new environment in the United States, we were ready to take on jobs that were below our skills sets.

It took my wife 3 months to get a job as a clerk, but I was unemployed longer, for a year. One can just imagine the anxiety we had to cope with during that period. There were times when I almost regretted coming here to the United States, but the die had been cast, so I was determined to persevere and survive in my new environment.

During that period of adjustment, we nearly exhausted our savings. Early on, I was hospitalized, at a time when I was still without work and health insurance. One night at the hospital cost us four thousand dollars. To insure independence in our movements as we desperately looked for work, we purchased two used cars, eating further into our savings. We availed of ad hoc health insurance for my wife and kids just so we could avoid a financial disaster if ever one of them got sick; I had a pre-existing health issue, so getting health insurance on my own was out of the question. I could only get it through my employer. We made sure that we took care of our children's basic needs even as our savings dwindled. And even when my wife and I were still unemployed, we shared in the household costs of our host family (my three unmarried sisters who were living in the same house), just to keep our self-respect afloat.

Our children were used to the liberal upbringing engendered by (us) their parents in our totally independent life in Jakarta, such that living with conservative aunts in the United States was an unwelcome regression to them. They were not used to the intrusion and the meddling that is customary in a multi-family traditional Filipino household even in the United States.

It was only a matter of time before the culture clash within our household would break out into the open, ultimately making us opt for the austere but independent life in a mobile home park, at the behest of our children. In November 2001, we used what remained of our savings to pay the down payment for a 1972 3-bedroom, 2-bathroom mobile home and take a 15-year mortgage that cost us $900 a month in payments, on top of the monthly space rent of $420. Fortunately, I was already working for the State of California at that time.

My wife and I got stuck in jobs that required probably a tenth of the skills we had honed through years of academic training and working as professionals. Our financial compensations were actually better in absolute terms compared to what we received in Jakarta, but the living expenses in Northern California near San Francisco were astronomical compared to our living expenses in Jakarta.

We missed the luxury of having three maids and two drivers in Jakarta; in our new environment, we were the maids and drivers for our family. It was made worse by the fact that our children had grown up in Jakarta with maids and drivers at their behest so that the task of keeping our house clean and organized in the United States fell into my wife's and my laps by default. I was in charge primarily for the laundry tasks, washing, drying, and ironing clothes, while my wife was commander-in-chief of kitchen affairs.

Even at the office, the tasks we performed were physically more and mentally less taxing than what we were used to. In Jakarta, I did not have to touch a computer; that task was relegated to the secretarial staff and my direct subordinates. I did a lot of thinking and discussing both with my bosses (the owners of the companies I worked for) and my subordinates. I hand-wrote my communications with external parties, both domestic and foreign, and the secretary would do all the other mechanical things to ensure that the communiqués were typed and sent to their destination. In the United States, the first thing I had to learn before being hired was working with computers; it took eight months before I became proficient in Microsoft Office applications like Word, Excel, Access, PowerPoint, and Publisher.

The point of this narrative is to underscore the fact that relocating to a new environment involves a lot of sacrifices. One has to continually tell oneself that the objective/s of the relocation far outweighs the difficulties of the adjustments. Our children needed my wife and myself to make that decision, regardless of the risks and the temporary hardships, because it opened new possibilities for them to improve on what my wife and myself already attained.

PART 7:
RUMINATIONS

CHAPTER 19

EXCITING THINGS TO DO AFTER RETIREMENT

I just turned 56 a month ago. It could be a milestone of some sort for some other person. For me, it just means nine more years of slogging it out--daily--here at the office before finally retiring at 65. Most people look forward to that day when they can finally rest their body, exhausted from the daily grind of cumbersome, oftentimes boring, and meaningless work. I, however, beg to differ from them.

I look forward to my own retirement, but for quite a different reason. I have been looking forward to it for some 10 years now, because it means for me graduating from semi-retirement--which is how I consider my current work now--to really exciting work that I have always wanted to do since I first started to work.

By exciting work I mean teaching. I imagine myself teaching young people--*pro bono*, because by then I will not need the income to live comfortably--about all the exciting things I have learned from life. I imagine myself teaching almost any subject, and enjoying it no end.

It will not matter how old my students are. I will always have something to teach kids about, be they elementary students, high school students, college students, or even graduate students. I believe I have amassed enough learning to last me another 40 years of pleasurable teaching. I smile when I think of the exciting possibilities awaiting me.

I would love to teach English Literature to high school kids the way I remember my third year high school teacher--an American priest who first got me interested in Shakespeare and Carl Sandburg--taught it to us, with passion and eloquence, far too infectious for my appreciative young mind. I would also love to teach Philosophy of Religion to college students, with far greater depth and insight than when I first taught it in 1971 and 1972. I would even love to teach Business Management, or Market Research, or thesis writing, the way I remembered my graduate school teachers taught us, no-holds-barred, candid, supportive, and without recrimination. I imagine myself like the Pied Piper, happily leading small kids on their path to learning, opening their young gullible eyes to the wonders of the possible, seeing their small unsophisticated eyes transfixed in awe as they listen to me discuss civilization's great strides. Yes, I imagine myself doing all these---during the happiest years of my lifetime.

I have always imagined myself wearing the sandals of Socrates, helping young minds navigate the maze of ideas through sharp questions I have crafted, happily observing them blaze their way through with the probity of their intellect--recklessly unafraid, my students and myself, as to where their bold endeavors would lead us--much like I had done in my early years. I had a taste of something like that twelve years ago in Indonesia where I taught in a graduate school for business. It was such an exhilarating experience that I want to savor it again.

That would be my third career, and hopefully, the most satisfying of all. It is certainly something worth looking forward to.

Teaching was my first career--a long time ago--when I was a young man in my twenties and just out of academe. It turned out to be short-lived—a little less than two years--not because it did not satisfy me, but because the people who had the power to let me flourish to my full potential as a teacher lacked the courage to stand up for me in my hour of need. In two consecutive years I lost my teaching load in two Catholic colleges. I was young, idealistic, and uncompromising, fitting the profile of the potential troublemaker. But I was also a very good teacher, according to student evaluations, one of the best in both schools.

Teaching was quite addictive. Even with the memory of undeserved terminations, I longed to be back in the campuses of my younger years. I did have several stints at teaching again, after I got my master's degree in business administration.

The first opportunity was to teach marketing subjects to full-time working but part-time studying young women at the Philippine Women's University.

The second opportunity to go back to teaching came from my best friend and former classmate who had become the chairman of the philosophy department in a Catholic College for women.

He offered me an experimental subject under philosophy titled Philosophy of Business. The subject was tailor-made for me, as I had both a master's degree in Philosophy and a master's degree in Business Administration. I was happy with the potential challenge of the subject, and I accepted. I tackled the subject with a gourmet's appetite, not wanting to fail my friend in his attempt to be philosophically adventuresome, also wanting to create for myself a reputation of being an innovative teacher-thinker. I enjoyed that year of teaching, being able to ask provocative questions that nobody else could ask because I could straddle, with license, the two worlds of philosophy and business.

It felt satisfying while it lasted, but I had to cut it short to a year because my other profession as marketing executive necessitated a change in my life plan.

CHAPTER 20

A BUSINESS BREAKTHROUGH

I t was a business everyone in the company did not want to have anything to do with.

The company owner's wife had become acquainted with the food supplement business in Australia. She was spending most of her time there where her children went to school and where they had built a house. Australians were crazy about food supplements, and it took just a few years before she got the bug herself. She contacted one Australian company that specialized in food supplements, and after several discussions with company officers, she persuaded her husband to start a franchise in Indonesia.

I was not in good terms with the company owner's wife, and so it seemed only natural that I would not be involved in the preparation for the launch of the Bullivants line of food supplements even though I was the marketing director of Brataco at the time. A bright, though inexperienced, young lady was assigned to manage the business. After the launch, the main activity was in-store. Some thirty young women were trained to sell the products in specialty stores in Jakarta, Bandung, and Surabaya. About twenty sales promo girls were posted in Jakarta specialty stores.

As with most new businesses where the products are imported, the main problem the young manager had to grapple with was stock management. The products they forecasted to sell well did not do very well while some that they underestimated did very well, resulting in a very unwieldy stock situation. To compound the problem, replenishment during the initial months was geared toward their flawed forecast, and that aggravated further the stock problem. By the end of the first year, many of the overstocked items were expiring while some items were chronically out of stock. The stock problem demoralized both the field force and the young manager, culminating in her decision to accept another company's offer to join them at a higher salary.

At the insistence of his wife, the owner hired a young male doctor to take over the management of the business, but the business continued to be plagued with problems. The stock management problem persisted while other problems surfaced. The young male doctor turned out to be an absentee executive who was seen in the office only twice a month, only at those times when the field force would hold their regular meetings. Payment of salaries and sales commissions was chronically delayed. The business group became the butt of jokes of the other business groups. Sales achievement was at half the sales target. Brataco did not make any money, and the foreign principal was unhappy. The business was just trudging along aimlessly. In everyone's mind, it was just a matter of time before the owner would pull the plug to formalize its death.

At some distance, I would at times take a sneak look at the business results, wondering why it was made to float along without being subjected to the usual stringent requirements demanded of the other healthier business units. I did this always with a detached feeling, as

I was not involved and had no intention to be involved. I knew that whoever managed the business would report to the owner's wife, and I personally could not stand her.

It was a complete surprise therefore when one fateful morning at ten the owner came up to my cubicle and casually informed me that from that day on I was to take charge of the food supplements business. I was to devote all my energy to reviving the business! And to make it less surreal, he added that they had just hired a marketing manager who would take over the businesses I was actively managing.

After the initial shock, I started to recover my focus. I was seething mad, but I was more determined to take the challenge and win the battle.

My first order of business was to learn as much as possible about our food supplements business. I went back to the basics. I tried to talk to the young doctor. I got the impression, however, that he did not want me to know very much about how he was managing it. He was always evasive and would not provide me with hard data that I could study and analyze. So I decided to compile my own database from what were available from the company's computer data records. I designed my own data tables and kept them handy in my own master clear book. I made lists, of the stores where we had sales promo girls, of sales promo girls and their assignments, of products, of specific items, and of many other things that I thought were worth knowing and analyzing.

I talked to the field force leader whom I found to be quite cooperative. She patiently explained to me how things were done, the problems they usually encountered, and the things that needed to be undertaken to improve the business operation. I specifically asked her for her views about their compensation scheme, and I gathered from her that the field force personnel all looked forward to some kind of an incentive scheme that would improve their compensation.

Relying on her invaluable insights, I designed a compensation scheme that we could try to implement. Basically, it consisted of giving them a base salary that every sales promo girl could live on, plus a generous commission scheme that was indexed on sales over a minimum sales target. Each store was given a minimum sales target. Sales over that would generate a 10% commission for the sales promo girl.

During the first three months of our trial run, the number of field persons that received commission dramatically increased, from three on the first month to five on the third month, out of twenty in Jakarta. The effect on the girls was dramatic. They started to believe that getting commissions was doable. By the tenth month, all the girls were getting commissions. The really good ones were reaching sales that were double their target.

In the meantime, the young doctor resigned, but at that point his presence was already irrelevant to the business. I took over direct management of the business in all aspects, assisted by the field force leader. I analyzed past sales by product item, and with it, I was able to fine-tune the stock replenishment system, so that by the eighth month I had finally stabilized our stock levels. I was communicating with the foreign principal by e-mail on a daily basis, and the foreign principal was a happy man. We were on a roll, and everybody was happy. I had expanded my Jakarta field force from twenty girls to thirty, and they were all surpassing their targets and earning commissions. I hired a young doctor as an assistant, and the field leader got her twenty percent salary raise. The owner, who had initially objected to the generous commission scheme of 10% on sales-over-target, was converted to my line of thinking as the records showed that for the first time in more than five years our food supplements business earned profits that year.

Even the financial guys in the company were amazed at the transformation of the business. For me, the more significant transformation happened to my people in the field force. I remembered meeting them when I first introduced myself to them; the people I saw had sad faces, were unsure of the future, postured with sagging shoulders. Eight months later, these same people had smiling faces, looking very confident, postured with shoulders raised high. More importantly for them, they had disposable income from the commission scheme to finance other needs.

It was probably the smallest business that I ever managed in my career. It was not even significant for Brataco as a business unit. For me, it was the most satisfying endeavor that I worked on.

Even my relationship with Rod, my counterpart at Bullivants, changed. Initially, he regarded me almost with contempt as one of the Brataco executives who did not give a damn about their business. This attitude was evident in our initial meetings in Jakarta. On my part, I initially thought he was one of those petulant principals who would constantly whine about how their business was being neglected by Brataco. As I got involved and started to make the necessary changes to make the business more viable, our relationship warmed up. The sales figures continued to improve dramatically. He started soliciting feedback from our field people about how things were going, and as responses continued to be positive, his attitude changed. We became good friends in the course of our working together. When he learned at the end of 1999 that I was leaving Brataco to migrate to the United States, he sent a fax to my boss the owner, expressing his praise for the work I had done for their business. Deliberately, he furnished me a copy, but at that time, I did not really need it. It was icing on the cake, pretty but not really that essential.

The most precious lesson I learned from that successful venture was that it is much easier to achieve an objective when everybody knows they have a stake in successfully reaching it. It is doubly enjoyable when you see your efforts spread some joy around as they share in the benefits of a successful undertaking.

Chapter 21

Religion and The Vending Machine

I n primitive time, when Gods were considered to be less than benevolent beings but more like spoiled brats who liked to have tantrums at the expense of men, religion generally consisted of pacifying the Gods, and one of these practices was offering sacrifices, including human sacrifices, to them. One example of this is in the Bible's Old Testament when--to test his loyalty--God asks Abraham to offer Isaac his son as sacrifice to Him.

In a sense, this idea of "pacifying" God has persisted to our day in the practice of religion, even though God is now regarded as a benevolent being and no longer a tantrum-prone spoiled brat. There is an underlying awareness of God's almighty power and man's abject position in relation to this powerful being. But there is slyness in man that attempts to make a fool of this powerful being.

God has now taken the form of a *spiritual* vending machine where men insert coins in the form of good deeds and prayers to ensure that only good things can happen to them. We men think that we can control God by bribing him, by buying his good graces with good deeds and prayers. And if something bad happens to us, we ascribe this to not having given God enough prayers and good deeds, as if God is like a plant that would wither without our showering it with prayers and good deeds.

When two boxers are in the ring just before a fight, it is not uncommon for both to pray to God for victory. In some sort of ridiculous situation, they both compete for his favor. Of course, one eventually comes out victorious, so he ascribes his victory to God's help. *God sided with him.* Perhaps it is worth asking: do we really think God had anything to do with that victory, or for that matter, with that fight? It does seem ridiculous, but that is the logical extension of our belief that God designs and controls everything; in our view, God determines who wins and who loses, and everything that happens, happens within his grand design of things. So, the logical response for our smart human minds is to try to manipulate God so that He serves us. We think that we can make God take our side, by bribing him with prayers and good deeds, so that he will intervene on our behalf.

Who now is the puppet, and who is the puppeteer? If God were as smart as we say He is, would He not see through our machinations to make Him comply with what we want? We treat this being that controls everything as if He is intellectually inferior to us as we manipulate him to serve us. Who are we to think that we can ultimately control him for our narrow objectives? We delude ourselves into thinking that we can influence God's thinking about things. If he is as wise as we say he is, then he thinks apart from our narrow and selfish wishes, and he alone understands in his righteous and all-knowing wisdom how things must be.

When a loved one is afflicted with a terminal disease, how should one talk to God without appearing as if one is asking a special favor? I ask this because about a year ago, my wife was diagnosed with 4th stage breast cancer. How do I pray to God without asking him to intervene in the affairs of the natural world for her? I would be lying if I tell you that I know. I believe that ultimately it is science that will determine whether my wife can beat her affliction. I believe that some cure is out there, within the reach of capable men, waiting to be discovered. The cure is within the affairs of the natural world where capable men have to drive themselves to discover the secrets of what is possible.

Yet, even as I believe that God is the ground of all being, I have to accept that nature and its laws, although discoverable and harness-able, can be harsh and unforgiving, that my wife is an ordinary human being subject to nature's laws and can die before a cure is discovered. I wish I can believe otherwise and live in a fool's paradise so that I can pray to God to intervene for me *because I am special.* The problem is: every one thinks of himself as special before God when everything else fails. How can I ask for myself something that is withheld from others---that is, supernatural intervention in the affairs of the natural world?

I have come to believe that God rules the world through his laws, the laws of nature. It is these laws that keep the regularities that we see in nature. The real meaning of God being the ground of being is that He is the cause of the regularity of things. The explanations of science are really His laws being discovered so that progress and technology are grounded in Him and can be understood as the unfolding of His grand design. Creation is a continuing process, and the exciting thing is that man is leading the process of discovering and harnessing, including the cures for cancer that my wife so desperately needs.

CHAPTER 22

JESUS' CRUCIFIXION
AND HIS HUMANITY

I t is quite difficult to reconcile the twin ideas that Jesus was both a true man and a true God. If he was a man, was he subject to the uncertainties that constantly plague every man? Did his being a man mean that he could not see the future and could only see the present?

If Jesus could clearly see the future, would there be any merit to his suffering and death? For if he could see with certainty what lay beyond his suffering and death, then his suffering was not any greater or nobler than an ordinary man's suffering because an ordinary man cannot see with certainty what lies ahead, beyond his current suffering and impending death.

If Jesus was the *ultimate role model*, he had to experience suffering the way every man undergoes suffering, replete with its attendant uncertainty of what lies beyond death. His eyes had to be "veiled" with regard to the future, for his suffering to have merit. If Jesus was a true man, he had to be subject to the conditions that befall every man. Otherwise, he was cheating, like taking a test while knowing the questions and the answers. There would be no merit in that.

Martin Scorsese's film, *The Last Temptation of Christ,* hit this difficult-to-understand mystery on the head. Scorsese's attempt to portray the humanity of Christ in plain terms-- in the context of how life would have been to an ordinary man who was struggling to understand an internal obsession he could not fully fathom--is powerfully clear and realistic. It was only after watching that film that I began to appreciate the implication of Jesus' being a true man. Jesus was truly a hero only if he was a true man.

Like any ordinary man, he had to trust that God exists, that he as man had a special mission, that his life had meaning even if it had to end by being crucified on the cross as a blasphemer of the highest order, lower than the lowest criminal. As he lay dying on the cross, he must have been plagued by doubts as to his own real worth, as his eyes continued to be veiled. Even if he were only a man, *not a true God,* he would still have been the greatest of men.

What is significant to me about Jesus is that he lived his life as a decent man, even as he confronted his own doubts during his hours of trial, abandoned by his friends when he needed them most. When everything was going against him, when he felt the one he called his father seemed to have abandoned him, he could still--with uncanny graciousness--say to the good thief that they would be together that day in Paradise.

I have often wondered what was the significance of the cross as a symbol for anybody who wanted to follow Jesus. Through the years, it has become a bit clearer. Jesus won through his crucifixion, not through his resurrection. When everything was dark, when there were no guarantees that he was right, he made that leap of faith--into the arms of the God he could not see. Notwithstanding his own uncertainty and doubts, he affirmed in his last breath as man the nobility of what he preached and blindly believed in.

The historical Jesus that was subject to all the limitations that humans are heir to has grown on me especially now that a rain of misfortunes have poured into my life because I can see him as my role model for coping with my misery.

CHAPTER 23

THE MYTH OF SISYPHUS

The Myth of Sisyphus is the title of a book written by Albert Camus, a French writer who was also an existentialist philosopher. He was a student of Jean Paul Sartre, the prominent French existentialist philosopher. For Camus, the story of Sisyphus mirrors the predicament of man.

For stealing something valuable from the Gods, Sisyphus was condemned to roll a big boulder up the mountain of Hades. When he reaches the top of the mountain, the boulder rolls down the mountain. From there, Sisyphus has to start rolling it up again.

For Camus, such is the life of man. Human life is essentially a futile effort. There is no meaningful goal for existence. Man exists to strive, but all that striving is meaningless because there is nothing at the end of that strife. There is no salvation, no light at the end of the tunnel. If there are Gods, then life is their big joke. They snicker at the striving of serious-minded men who think reaching the top of the mountain is a glorious accomplishment.

The search for meaning has always been a fascinating endeavor for thinking men. And the search for the meaning of life is as intriguing as it is exciting. If human life is a pointless exercise that amounts to nothing, does it not make sense that, instead of hating it, we should make it a nice experience as we go through it? *It does not matter what is at the end.* What should matter is what we do before we reach the end. If life is a big joke, then let us make it a good and enjoyable joke. If life is nothing but striving that leads nowhere, then let us enjoy the striving while it lasts. Let us avenge ourselves at the Gods *by savoring the strife.*

That is exactly how most of the existentialists regard life. Because there is no heaven to look forward to, then we should create heaven on earth. The existentialist is committed to this life because there is no other life. This life is not a vale of tears after which we get our reward. This life is our reward. It is here for us to make it great and make it an enjoyable experience. It is a challenge of limitless proportions for kindred souls to transform this earth into a new heaven. Within this context, the next phase of the evolutionary process is for men with boundless energy, unfettered by the idea of an after-life, to create a new earth fashioned after their visions of heaven.

As a young man, I was enamored by Camus' nihilist heroism especially in contrast to the Catholic Church's usually phlegmatic response to real problems in the world. It seemed to me then that the atheists, like Camus, Sartre, and Nietzsche, were winning the war to make the earth a better place.

CHAPTER 24

NOSEBLEED

In the late 1960s when I was in my late teens in the Philippines, there were a lot of students who liked to be considered student activists. Their primary activities as activists were attending teach-ins and joining other students in protest rallies. It was the fad of that era to be known as a young person who cared about the problems of the country to such an extent that one would risk even one's life for one's ideals.

Although I was relatively isolated most of the time in the rustic highlands of Cavite province where I was studying for the priesthood, I was one of those seminarians who were permitted by seminary authorities to occasionally leave the confines of the seminary and mix with farmers and student activists in teach-ins and rallies elsewhere. Like the other seminarians in our seminary that did what was euphemistically called *social work*, I was quite proud to be known as a student activist. It was the mark of someone who had no vested interests to protect and personally fearless

The primary activity of the activist seminarian was slightly different from our student activist counterparts in Metropolitan Manila. We socialized with farmers who were living near the seminary by spending most of our free time visiting our farmer friends in their houses, sometimes slipping out of the seminary campus after lights out to hang out with our farmer friends, just telling stories and drinking coffee late into the night. Our activist mentors taught us that spending time with the farmers was important because it ultimately engendered personal empathy on our part. We started to see things from the farmers' perspective gradually. It helped bridge the gap between the middle-class minded seminarian and the simple-minded lowly farmer. This was the basic conversion strategy to develop intellectuals into dedicated sympathizers of the farmers. It worked well with me.

Unfortunately, I was made to leave the seminary 4 years before I would have been ordained as a priest. For two successive years, the two colleges where I taught Philosophy after leaving the seminary terminated my services. I carried the stigma of being a potential troublemaker whenever they discovered who I was and where I came from.

I finally decided to lie low to be able to survive in the unprotected world outside the moral walls of the seminary. I still had the same ideas as before, but I just kept them to myself. I concentrated on developing my other skills and talents, and I thrived as a business executive both in the Philippines where I worked for 8 years after my teaching stint and in Indonesia where I worked for 18 years. It was in Indonesia where I finally discarded my uncertainties about my capabilities as a business executive and became comfortable with myself as a professional. I took on all kinds of challenges successfully until there was nothing to prove anymore.

I came to the United States to start a new life at 51 as a semi-retired government employee, away from the rat race of my younger years. It was as a state employee of California that I met my good friend Larry, an African American alumnus of UCLA, who has been my lunch buddy and my conversation partner in the last 5 years. We hit it off quite well early on as we discovered that we were interested in a lot of similar things. In answer to his probing questions, I dug deep into my memory and excavated the ideas and emotions of my youth that had lay dormant there. Suddenly, it was exciting again for me to talk about Nietszche, Camus, Hans Kung, and Edward Schillebeeckx.

Larry has a characteristic doggedness in his questioning that riles people who do not understand where he is coming from. It is part of his honest pursuit of truth not to be content with run-of-the-mill answers to his well-thought-out questions. When he asks difficult questions, he expects earnest answers, not platitudes. Larry's tough and uncompromising questions compelled me to search for the books of my activist youth, rediscovering old themes that fascinated me in the past. I had to re-read some of those books that I read thirty years earlier as well as new ones by the same authors. I had to think back and remember the lessons taught by the one mentor who taught us the concepts of *immanence*, *transcendence*, and *eschatology*.

I re-discovered the dreams of my youth, and at the same time, I felt guilty about my lying low in the past to survive. I had friends who had died and some who suffered because they would not keep quiet, and I had conveniently left the world of activism to survive anonymously, hiding in plain sight, even though my conscience directed me elsewhere.

As if from a deep slumber, I gradually woke up and trekked back to the world of the activist. This was my way of atoning for my sin of omission. At 51, I began by attending union activities and becoming a union steward at my work site. I graduated into walking precincts during elections as well as phone banking for progressive candidates. I volunteered my time whenever I could for progressive causes. I became a regular at activist functions so that advocacy organizations started calling me for other activities. I also became active in my neighborhood, taking up residents' issues in the mobile home park where I live. At times, I would forgo my weekend rest because a campaign needed boots on the ground urgently. Even as my physical stamina and agility waned, I discovered I had new strengths derived from well-developed skills honed through years of constant practice and experimentation.

I learned the power of words. By volunteering to read on Saturdays in the Catholic chapel where I attend mass, I experimented on how to optimize the delivery of the written word in a public forum. Through constant practice, I mastered that medium. Also through constant practice, I learned to craft words and use them to full impact. I wrote and wrote and wrote until I could feel like a master of the written word. I also discovered that even though words are influential in swaying people to take positions, they are basically cheap because at crunch time, *actions are more powerful.*

In the words of my friend Larry, those actions that oftentimes make your nose bleed are the ones that ultimately determine outcomes in the real world. It is the lonely actions of the activist who pounds the pavements with his boots and knocks on doors until residents cannot stand the noise anymore that make the vacillating voter dress up and go to the precinct to vote for the candidate that will really change things for the better. It is the activist in the work site who engages hostile colleagues in meaningful and respectful discussions to convert the unbelieving cynic to an active sympathizer that makes the labor union effective in that workplace.

It is not the fiery speeches delivered in plenary meetings, evoking enthusiastic applause that makes the organization strong. Rather, it is the patient efforts of the activist who takes on one-on-one conversations with his colleagues, and the patient actions of the union steward to represent troubled members at the workplace that ultimately make the organization strong, away from the fanfare of self-glorifying fiery speeches. The laying of a brick on top of another, *the tedious work that makes the nose bleed*, is what gives the organization its real strength.

CHAPTER 25

ANGELS OF GOD

There was a time when I was really angry with God because it seemed that He would always put me in very difficult situations to test me. Although I always delivered for Him, in many of those instances, my being true to Him would cost me, in terms of inconvenience, pain, and even loss of pride.

It got to a point where I would look around and would feel lonely because it seemed as if I was alone doing God's bidding, and instead of lightening my load, God would pile it up some more. I looked at the other people around me, and they seemed to be enjoying themselves, oblivious of the self-imposed responsibilities I had taken upon myself for my belief in God.

Slowly, my indignation grew. Why was I carrying the world's burden disproportionately? Why did God make me conscious of my responsibilities to the extent that I was not enjoying my life as much as the other people around me? Why was I being good when most people did not care? Why was I chosen to carry the brunt of being righteous in a world where conscienceless people could use all their guile and win? Because I tried to follow God's rules, I often ended as the tail-ender. Success seemed to be always beyond me because I tried to always follow the rules. Because I tried to live my life within the context of *good-and-evil*, I was not up to the machinations of people who lived their lives in the context of *what-works* and *what-is-expedient-and-effective*. I felt totally impotent in a potency-driven world that regarded me a failure on its terms.

My prayers turned to cries of complaint. I fought with God in my mind. I asked Him for temporary relief of one to two years from the stringent life I was living. I wanted to stop being Mr. Good Guy for a while. I wanted to experience the life of a man without God.

Up to that time, I believed I was a self-made man. Despite having Diabetes, I had subjected myself to physical rigors only a man with uncanny self-discipline would undergo, to put myself in tip-top physical shape. I went to the fitness center thrice a week and played basketball on Sunday afternoons. I always spent long hours whenever I was preparing for examinations that tested not only mental acumen but also complete grasp of the material to be tested, not leaving anything to chance. I was always ready to help out anybody who needed my help, without waiting for any form of compensation. In my mind, I could truly face God and tell Him to His face that I had served Him to the best of my ability. Yet, He had not made it easy for me. I could think of so many instances when He was the one who failed me. I honestly thought He was the one who owed me, rather than myself owing Him.

To add insult to injury, I had a heart attack when I thought I was at the prime of my physical health. Ironically, I had it while playing basketball on a Sunday afternoon. While I was being wheeled into the intensive care unit of the hospital in Jakarta, the nurses who could see my muscular half-naked body could not believe I just had a heart attack. It was so untypical that a relatively young man at forty-three, living a physically healthy life style, would succumb to heart attack. After being in the hospital for four weeks, I was discharged with a clean bill of health because I passed all the subsequent tests that I was subjected to.

The next two years, I could feel my health deteriorating fast. All that time, I was angrier with God because I believed that what happened to me was His devious plan to quell my budding rebellion. I moped and brooded because I really could not do anything about it. Finally, my cardiologist decided to do an angiogram on my heart, a procedure where they insert a catheter through a major blood vessel and take a peek at the arteries in the heart. The verdict was conclusive: I had blockages of 100%, 80%, and 70% on three major arteries in my heart. About a quarter of my heart was permanently damaged by the heart attack two years earlier. I was four weeks away from a major heart attack that could be fatal. I needed a heart bypass surgery quickly.

In my panic, I accelerated all the preparations for a heart bypass surgery. Taking the word of a local cardiologist in Jakarta that his surgeon friend in Perth, Australia, could perform the surgery at a moment's notice, my wife and I flew to Perth in a hurry, leaving our three children under the care of some friends. The thoracic surgeon was Mark Edwards. He was livid when we told him about his cardiologist friend's words. He said he was fully booked four weeks in advance. He advised me to come back after four weeks. Thinking that I was being condemned to death by default, I pleaded with him to place me in his proximate schedule.

I must have looked so desperate as he looked at me with his sad–looking eyes. He heaved a sigh and announced that he was scheduling me for surgery that Saturday, even before he had a chance to tell his wife and kids about the weekend he would not be with them and even before he could call together his weekend surgical team. I did not know him from Adam, but this man decided in a couple of seconds what I would owe him for the rest of my life.

There was another man in that consultation room. His name was Paul Sarmidi. He was the person my boss in Jakarta contacted to make the arrangements for my surgery in Perth. He was a small dealer of canned goods that our company was using as distributor of our food products for Perth, a secondary city located in West Australia with a population of one million. He had made the consultation arrangement with Mark Edwards. Paul Sarmidi was a radiologist during his prime years as a doctor in Jakarta, Indonesia; he was spending his years of retirement in Perth, West Australia. Chinese in ethnic origin, he was born and raised in Jakarta. He was what people generally called Chinese Indonesian.

Mark Edwards carried out a successful double-bypass heart surgery on me some fourteen years ago. Among the four patients from Indonesia that he successfully operated on at about the same week, I am the only one still alive today. Two died within a year after their surgeries, while the third one died within the third year after his surgery.

I stayed in Perth a total of two months for that surgery. I overstayed in Perth for a month because my official travel documents were stolen from the apartment hotel's safe, and it took some time for the Philippine Embassy in Canberra, Australia, to replace my documents.

Paul Sarmidi visited me every day I was there during those two months. All that my boss in Jakarta wanted from him was to make the initial arrangements for me. I also did not know him from Adam. He did not have to do what he did for me, but there was a genuine gentleness about Paul that I could not really fathom.

Slowly, I realized what was happening. What Mark and Paul did for me was more than just bring me back from the jaws of death; *they gave me new eyes.* I had always thought of myself as an exceptional man who was always ready to be the man God could count on to deliver for those who needed some help, and I begrudged Him for always putting me on the spot. When Mark and Paul delivered for me at the hour of my need, I was humbled by the message God seemed to be delivering.

It was as if He was telling me that all those talents that I considered to be mine were really His gifts to me, that all those opportunities to help were also His gifts to me, that I was one of the few He would call on because there were not many of us who could do those things for Him. By revealing to me two of his angels at the time of my need, he made me realize that *I was not alone in carrying out the things He wanted done.* There were other people like me, and I was in the company of great people who silently make the world a better place. Things did not look the same again afterwards. Forwards and backwards, I had a completely different view of things.

I began to understand that I was the lucky one. He had equipped me with all these things that other people needed, so that when they called out for help, I just happened to be around to be of help. I also began to understand that He intervenes in the daily affairs of the world through ordinary people like me who, feeling His immanent presence deep down in themselves, transform this world silently in small increments, almost unnoticeably. There are no big bangs to herald His miracles, just the quiet, whispered thanks of a needy person helped.

PART 8:
TRYING TIMES

CHAPTER 26

LIVING WITH A TERMINALLY ILL WIFE

As I write this, it has been seven months since my wife Del died of breast cancer.

Two weeks before her death, the two of us had celebrated our 26th wedding anniversary in a very simple way at the Starbucks near our house by ordering muffins and coffee. Her breast cancer, diagnosed 25 months earlier to be in its fourth stage, had already traveled to her liver, brain, and lungs, but we were both still acting as if she was going to last a few more years. Nothing was sad about that anniversary celebration; we were enjoying something simple but meaningful for the two of us.

We had just reached one of our major goalposts two months earlier with the graduation of our eldest son Hamlet from Stanford with a double degree in Economics and International Relations. The next goalpost seemed reasonably within reach; our second son Voltaire was scheduled to graduate in eight months with a degree in Psychology from the University of Southern California. We were planning to be there for his graduation.

Tragic events always happen at the most inconvenient time. My wife's death came three weeks after Voltaire went back to school for his last year in college and two days after I brought my youngest child Lara to her boarding high school in Pebble Beach, some 100 hundred miles south from where we live. I suppose there is no such thing as convenient when faced with serious illness and death. We wish that circumstances were different, but we accept and adapt.

Del was diagnosed as having 4th stage cancer on the same day we received news that my older brother had died of drowning at Lake Berryessa in Napa Valley. The double blow would have been shocking to everybody affected so she kept the news of her ailment until after my brother's burial. My wife, my three children, and myself had an emotional crying session to mark her revelation that her ailment was terminal. It lasted two hours. Then, almost surreally, everything seemed to return to normal.

Del kept on working at UPS even after the revelation for another six months, taking off only to attend her weekly chemotherapy sessions. I took off from work every chemotherapy day to be with her, not really doing anything but drive her to the clinic and sit beside her during the session. I wished I could do more for her, but I was relegated by the circumstances to the most innocuous presence imaginable, but it was important for her that I was there, even when all I was doing was filling crossword puzzles to while away the time. I was a bit surprised that the oncology clinic did not exhibit a more foreboding gloom that one would expect to find in a place of desperate patients. The prevailing mood of the place was light, the nurses and the doctors with ready smiles at a moment's notice. The place could have passed for the foyer of heaven.

Del and I maintained much the same lightness that we witnessed at the clinic. She always exhibited a brave and hopeful face, even when the news about her ailment was worse than the previous one, and it was always progressively worse than the previous one. We always talked about things and plans as if we were going to be together for a long time. It was probably for each other's consumption. The possibility of her death was probably hovering over us, but we always kept it away from our conversations, probably because it would not have helped anyway, and we wanted to enjoy every moment we had for as long as it lasted, without brooding about the dire possibilities of the future.

Del took on every treatment that her doctor recommended with such enthusiasm and fortitude that I was always left wondering where she was getting the strength to cheerfully carry on. As her physical appearance changed drastically, with her hair falling off after brain radiation, and her body bulking up with her continuous use of steroids to mask the pain that the cancer in her brain was causing, I continually tried to remember how she looked before she became terminally sick. Physically she was not a pretty sight, but the personal qualities that she exhibited as she continued to face bravely her ailment and her anxieties, continually putting up a calm and happy face, brought me back to some thirty years earlier and made me remember why I became fascinated with her. She was exhibiting again the remarkable woman I met in my youth, the woman I fell in love with and decided to marry.

The last twenty-four months of our marriage were our happiest ones. Even an ailment as devastating as cancer brings with it some hidden gifts. We became more sensitive to each other's feelings, always trying to please each other, almost obsequiously. She was continually decorating our mobile home, tidying and tying up all the loose ends just in case she would not be around to do these. She was devising up all these projects to improve our house and create a garden that was the envy of our neighborhood. She found an incredible source of creative energy that amazed her friends who regularly visited her, my sisters who nightly supplied us with dinner, and me who continually saw these bursts of creative genius from an unknown source within her on a daily basis. It was as if this was her way of fighting whatever was killing her, telling it in her indefatigable way she was still in control of her life.

We planned together our daughter Lara's attempt to obtain a scholarship from the top boarding high schools in California, and we succeeded, receiving an annual grant of several thousand dollars for the next four years of her high school life. Lara was accepted to the boarding high school of her choice, at a minimal expense to our family. This was actually an essential part of our plan to keep her away from our house where for two years she had witnessed the ebbs and flows of her mom's health, something that we thought was not healthy for a young girl just in her teens. Lara's success in getting into a boarding school was a bittersweet pill for us; it was good for her emotionally, but we would miss our baby girl terribly. We knew this was the start of her weaning away from her parents. She would be back during summer and other shorter vacations, but she would not be coming back the way we always had her in the past.

Our second son Voltaire was his mom's baby boy. He had always been very close to his mom, and she would be excited every time he was scheduled to go home, even if for only a few days. He was our weird child, very creative, but also never quite mature for his age. He had learned a lot about the practical aspects of life by being far away from our protective clutches down there in Los Angeles. He would regale his mom with stories about his dates with pretty girls and his adventures and misadventures in his campus. He still had his weird friends around him, and he still dressed like the campus tramp, his uncombed hair worn long for at least a year, his beard unshaven for weeks, and his rubber shoes and khaki pants taped with black electric tape, making us wonder how he could coax those pretty girls to date him. His mom was completely satisfied with his development away from home, and we were seeing his good qualities—his generosity, his creativity—far outweigh his eccentricities, making me a convert to his mom's positive outlook for him.

Del's terminal illness brought home to the two of us the sense that life is too short to waste on the unimportant. We could be philosophical about a lot of things, because we both knew she was on borrowed time, and every new day was a gift to enjoy. We were relieved of the immediate concerns for daily survival because daily survival was much more real in our family; we were not as much concerned about holding on to our jobs and losing our pensions as we were about holding on to each other a little bit longer. There were times when I would be talking to her in person yet could already feel in my heart a great sense of loss, because I knew there would be a time when I would look and she would not be there in front of me.

I was in her room at the hospital when she finally left. There were no dramatic good-byes, just the attending nurse finding to her surprise that the patient had gone quietly without our noticing it. I had been told a few days earlier that she had only days to live. It was probably more difficult for our children than for me. I had been saying good-bye to her daily for twenty-five months through the unnoticeable nonverbal signals we had been sending each other throughout that terrible but glorious period of our married life.

CHAPTER 27

HITTING THE
BOTTOM OF THE BARREL

Eighteen months after I buried my wife, a mix of ailments afflicted me that have kept me bedridden for six months now.

The first indication that something was wrong happened during the months of January and February 2009 when I was inordinately sleeping off my entire weekends. I initially thought it was a good thing as I thought I was catching up with much-needed rest. I started to be alarmed when during longer weekends of three and four days made possible by public holidays, I kept on sleeping like I had become addicted to it.

Real trouble started when I began vomiting at the office for no apparent reason, forcing me to go home in the middle of a workday. At about the same time, I developed chest pain on both my right and left sides; I knew from experience that the pain was skin-deep, unrelated to any heart or lung problem. I did not think that these were serious, but just to be safe, I scheduled an appointment with my primary doctor who, after hearing my story and checking me, ordered a chest x-ray and blood lab tests. The x-ray result came back ten minutes later indicating no problem. Since the blood test results would be available only after an hour, my doctor sent me home with the promise that she would contact me if something significant came up.

Thirty minutes after I reached home, my primary doctor called asking me to immediately proceed to the office of a nephrologist as there were indications that my kidneys were not functioning well.

The nephrologist looked at me, and with somber eyes, declared, " Mr. Abaya, I don't know how you usually look, but from my perspective, you are a very sick man." He informed me that my creatinine level was extraordinarily high at 6.2 while normal level is only 1.0, indicating that my kidneys had shut down. He proceeded to tell me that he had looked at my medications and concluded that some of them had to be discontinued in order not to aggravate my condition. He tried to have me admitted to the hospital where he practices that afternoon, but my health insurance was not acceptable to the hospital so he decided to just let me stay at home on the condition that somebody among my relatives would be nearby 24 hours a day to make sure I would not pass away in my sleep. He told me to drink a lot of water, prescribed an acid reflux medicine for my vomiting problem, and scheduled weekly visits with him preceded by blood tests to specifically monitor my creatinine level.

Subsequent visits with my nephrologist indicated that my creatinine level was not significantly decreasing. He then proceeded to discuss with me the distinct possibility that I would have to undergo dialysis for the rest of my life. I was shocked at hearing this new information as I was really expecting that my kidney shutdown was only temporary. I was devastated to hear that I was entering such a life-altering condition.

It was about this time when my primary doctor called me up one night to inform me that she had referred my case and the lab test results to a team of oncology doctors. Based on their preliminary analysis, they suspected that I had multiple myeloma, a kind of cancer that attacks the bone marrow. She scheduled an appointment with one of the oncologists who explained to me what the disease was all about and who then proceeded to conduct a biopsy of my bone marrow by drawing bone marrow from me through the upper part of my buttocks. A week later, he called to inform me that I had indeed multiple myeloma. It was one of those hard blows that made me cry.

Five weeks after the onset of my health problems, one more was added. Painful blisters appeared on the left side of my front and back torso. Lying down on the bed became an agonizing exercise. I showed the blisters to my primary doctor who informed me that this was *shingles*, a disease that attacks the nerves and caused by a virus that had stayed in the body as a residue of having had chicken pox in early life. The blisters were both itchy and excruciatingly painful. I would lie in bed at night when painful attacks would usually happen, and in my desperation I would run around the house like a headless chicken until the morning. At times, the pain was so unbearable that I wished I could escape from my body. Even with my siblings' daily care of cleaning the blisters with hydrogen peroxide and applying antibiotics on them while I orally took anti-viral medicine, it took six weeks to dry up the blisters. Those were six long weeks of agony and despair, like being in a dark tunnel and not seeing any light, however minuscule. The painkiller Vicodin was of no help in easing the pain throughout this painful ordeal. Towards the end of this six-week period, I was at my wits' end when I told my oncologist about my untenable situation. He then prescribed a painkiller that specifically targets nerves; that reduced the pain to a third of the original level, an immense consolation even if it did not wipe away the pain altogether. I imagined that the pain would disappear once the blisters had completely healed, but I was terribly wrong. Even now, I still take the nerve-targeting painkiller, some three months after the blisters had healed. I can best describe the pain from that episode in my life when I had shingles as being *unrelentingly scourged by God*, and people who had it concur with my description.

Even with the shingles, my oncologist proceeded with the multiple myeloma treatment. As I was physically weakened, I underwent blood transfusion twice. The nurses also injected me four times with a special medicine to boost my blood count. Then the real treatment began where I would be subjected to several courses of treatment with the medicine Velcade, each course consisting of three weeks where during the first two weeks I received treatment twice a week and on the third week I met with my oncologist to evaluate the results.

I was practically bedridden during this period, taking time out only to meet with doctors and visit the labs for the regular blood draws ordered by my nephrologist and oncologist. I had bowel movement swings, from constipation to diarrhea, all in a week's period. I took a stool softener twice a day to deal with constipation and *imodium* when it went the other way. At home I used my legs quite sparingly as I was lying in bed most of the time, standing up only to go to the bathroom; this disuse of my legs weakened them substantially such that at some time I needed a cane to keep me from falling down as my legs could no longer support my body weight.

There were quite a number of times when I succumbed to self-pity. I would wake up at night and sob inconsolably. The barrage of blows that were thrown my way seemed endless and unrelenting. I tried making sense of what was happening to me, but it was difficult to see through the maze.

I remembered Job's story from the Old Testament. I told my best friend at the office who regularly called to see how I was doing that I felt God was pushing me to the limit, and I was almost tempted to give up in my desperation.

I knew that blaming God for what I was experiencing was the easiest way out, but *my better judgment knew it would be a cheap shot.* I had always believed that God does not choose who should suffer and who should not. He had put things in motion through the natural laws that he devised through His creative power, and the rest of reality follows a random process where some people get a disproportionate share of misfortunes. I am one of those, but God did not choose me.

This was brought home to me through my frequent visits to the oncology center for my treatment, the same oncology center where I accompanied my wife for two years before she passed away. I looked at the faces of the other patients, and *I did not see any anger.* We were all trying to cope with what were thrown our way. I could not complain about my misery without feeling like a *selfish elitist coward.* I could not bring myself to ask to be exempted from that misery. I felt I had no right to be treated differently than the other cancer patients. How could I ask for myself something that is not being given to the other cancer patients?

When one has reached the bottom of the barrel as I have, when everything seems bleak, one has to look at the brighter side of one's situation. Then one will see as I have the true meaning of *hope, love,* and *faith.*

I look at the eyes of the other cancer patients at the oncology center, and I am awed because *everybody without exception looks hopeful.* We all look forward to having our threatened lives extended a little bit more, maybe a year, two years, even five years. For each of us undergoing cancer treatment, hope springs eternal; *we know how it is to hope.* There are no guarantees for us, but *having hope* is enough to sustain us.

I experience a lot of *love* around me during these trying times. My siblings, especially my sisters, have been taking care of me, sleeping in the couches in my house overnight to make sure I can get some help if I needed one during the night, preparing my breakfast in the mornings as well my dinner in the evenings. My sons take turns in driving me to my many appointments. My best friend at the office has been very helpful in helping me get the necessary forms from the office and having these signed by the right people at the office; he has not tired of regularly calling me to get an update on my situation. My new wife, who arrived in March 2009 after a year's wait (as my fiancee) at the onset of my health problems, has been dutifully taking care of me during the day and accompanying me to my appointments, practically serving as my personal secretary; she was my girlfriend some 30 years ago whom I had dumped in favor of my first wife. The attitude of all the doctors and nurses who cheerfully and competently attend to me proves to me that the immanent God works his love through these hitherto-strangers in my life. Friends from the church where I serve as lector keep me in their prayers. One does not realize how much love is all around him until one reaches the bottom. I have found a lot of warm company there.

How does *faith* come into play in my situation? My belief that ultimately life is fair even when things become onerously unbearable has sustained me through this whole ordeal. I have come to accept the randomness that living on earth entails. It does not really matter what things happen to us; what matters is how we manage those things given our *faith* in God's fairness. *I no longer pray to God with my words; I am doing it with my life.*

I know I am dying, but we are all dying in one way or another. I do not know how far my bout with cancer will drag me. What I have learned through this ordeal is that one does not really get to know how strong or weak his convictions are until these are severely tested. *When we are reduced to the bare minimum, then we can see our glaring weaknesses as well as our hidden strengths under the spotlights of despair and faith.* This brings us to confront our true self without the veils of self-posturing and self-illusion. I am almost thankful for having undergone this ordeal.